THE
NEW MAGA
DEAL

THE
NEW MAGA
DEAL

The Unofficial Deplorables Guide
to Donald Trump's 2024 Policy Platform

PETER NAVARRO

With Contributions From:

Greg Autry • Stephen K. Bannon • David Bernhardt

Mike Davis • James Fanell • Frank Gaffney • Richard Grenell

Dr. Steven Hatfill • Mark Morgan • Bradley Thayer

Russ Vought • Dave Walsh

WINNING TEAM
PUBLISHING

To the Deplorables of Trump's America who build our roads and bridges, toil in our factories, and till our fields.

To the families of Trump's America who have woken up to woke nonsense and want nothing more than a world in which family values once again mean family values.

To our brave men and women in uniform who shall never again become cannon fodder in endless, unjust wars.

To all those in Trump's America who must have the right to bear arms, speak freely, and assemble peaceably without fear of a partisan and weaponized government out for retribution.

To Donald John Trump himself, who carries our burdens for us and is willing to risk it all to save us all.

Contents

Foreword   xi

Introduction   xv

1. The MAGA Messaging Imperative and Policy Agenda   1

2. The ACTION, ACTION, ACTION Plan to Take Back Trump's America   9

3. The Buy American, Hire American Imperative   13

4. An America First Budget Will Turn Us Back from the Fiscal Cliff   17

5. President Trump Will Unwind the Follies of Bidenomics   21

6. Defending American Jobs Through Fair, Balanced, and Reciprocal Trade   25

7. Decoupling the U.S. Economy from a Cheating Communist China   31

8. America's Pension Funds and IRAs Must Stop Funding the Chinese Military   37

9. A Bidenomics March to Strategic Energy Subservience   41

10. The Critical Importance of American Strategic Electricity Dominance   45

11. Your Volvo May Be a Chinese Spy   51

12. Toward a Rational Federal Lands Policy and Return to Strategic Energy Dominance   55

CONTENTS

13. The Crisis at Our Southern Border   59

14. Securing Our Borders: Every Town in America Is Now a Border Town   67

15. Stopping the Deadly Flood of Communist Chinese Fentanyl   73

16. Declaring War on the Drug Cartels and Child Traffickers   77

17. Disarming a Weaponized Department of (In)Justice and FBI   83

18. The 2024 Presidential Election as a Referendum on Whether to Imprison Donald Trump   87

19. Defending Our Constitutional Judiciary   91

20. Freeing the J6 Prisoners   95

21. Ensuring Free, Honest, and Fair Elections and Election Integrity   99

22. Eradicating Forced Vaccinations and Holding Mainstream Media Liable for Deadly Misreporting   105

23. Cleaning DEI out of Academia   111

24. Donald Trump Will Hold Communist China and Anthony Fauci Accountable for COVID-19   117

25. Reading, Writing, and Arithmetic—Not Wokeness in School Curricula   121

26. Protecting Parents' Rights and the Right to Choose Their Children's Schools   127

27. Just Say Double No to Sex-Change Operations for Children   133

CONTENTS

28. President Trump Will Save Women's Sports   137

29. President Trump Will Make America Healthy Again   141

30. Breaking Up Big Tech and Its Billionaire Oligarchs   145

31. Stop E-Commerce from Inundating American Households with Counterfeits!   151

32. Cracking Down on the "Wokefare" of American Corporations   157

33. President Trump Will Cancel "Cancel Culture" in Our K–12 Schools, Colleges, and Universities   161

34. Communist China's Cyber Attacks Must Be Declared Acts of War   167

35. Protecting Taiwan's Strategic Value to the United States   171

36. The Trump "America First" Doctrine of Foreign Policy Must Be Restored in 2025   177

37. America Shall Not Sleep by the Light of a Communist Chinese Moon   185

Epilogue   189

Concluding Thoughts   195

Author's Note   197

Appendix A   203

Appendix B   209

Foreword

by Stephen K. Bannon

It's dawn in New York City. With only a few hours of sleep, I am glued to my iPad, Bloomberg blasting on the TV, phone cupped to my ear as I'm talking to hedge fund associates in London. The news is bleak. Global capital markets are imploding on the over-hyped information war as the corporate business news networks react with complete panic at the election of the new leader of the free world: Donald J. Trump.

A few short hours before, 2:30 a.m. EST on November 9, 2016, the Associated Press' vote tally declared Michigan, Wisconsin, and Pennsylvania for Trump, making him the first Republican since President Ronald Reagan in 1980 to pierce the Democrat "blue wall" of the industrial heart of the Midwest. That act made Trump president-elect of the United States.

The news of that success stunned the nation and the world. On election night at our headquarters in New York, our campaign staff was glued to eight television sets, as almost every mainstream media anchor looked ashen and shocked at Trump's looming win. But now, it was, again, morning in America. No one was more alarmed than the financial overlords that control the true levers of power, from Wall Street to the city of London.

To say they were unhappy is an understatement. That ill humor manifested itself in an across the board sell-off of every asset class. There was a "sharp sell-off overnight in Asia" reported by the *New York Times.* "Futures of the S&P 500 stock market plunged 5%."

It was not the fact that President-Elect Trump was not a respected businessman. He was. But he ran as a fire-breathing Populist and an economic Nationalist. The uncertainty of whether his policies would match his rhetoric, and the uncertainty of whether these policies would actually work in the world of the "postwar international rules-based order" was the question of the morning. Trump's victory was the greatest comeback in American political history, defeating not simply the Clinton Mafia but the neoliberal neocon policies she embodied.

Flipping channels, I came to the most pro-Clinton, pro-establishment, pro-elite channel—CNBC and its show *Squawk Box.* Before my eyes sat the architect of the Trump campaign's intellectual foundation on trade, manufacturing, and all things China: Dr. Peter Navarro. And he was getting hammered by a full attack mode of the Democratic anchors of the show.

But that hammering soon turned to hushed silence as Dr. Navarro, using all his Harvard PhD in economics lingo, combined with street smarts gleaned from years of actual investing, turned the guns around. Tax cuts, tariffs, manufacturing renaissance—growth, growth, growth. The animal spirits of capitalism unleashed as only America can do. And all of it in Trump Time—not tomorrow but today, not later but now, not talk but action.

Dr. Navarro's prescription began with cutting taxes for all Americans and cutting corporate taxes to 15 percent. That's a bullish increase in net earnings. Next was a moratorium on all new regulations that don't threaten public health and safety. Common sense, and a pure Reagan supply side effect that lowers costs.

And more common sense; stop the war on oil, natural gas, shale, and clean coal, making American companies more competitive. Kill the regulatory burdens that have been killing American prosperity.

Of course, Dr. Navarro had it exactly right. The Dow reached 25,000 just fourteen months later on January 4, 2018, and hit 30,000 when the policies took root.

Immediately, things turned around.

This extraordinary individual—the toughest, most dedicated fighter in President Trump's first term—has brought forth a book about those very policies. The knowledge presented within these covers has come at a steep price—the overwhelming pushback from the Administrative State. Needless to say, they are not fans of Dr. Navarro and are sworn enemies to MAGA, to America First, and to Donald Trump.

The converging of the crisis of the invasion of America; the exploding national debt; and the conflicts in Ukraine, the Middle East, and Taiwan will make the early days of President Trump's second term even more perilous than his first. Immediate action will be necessary—thank Divine Providence that Donald J. Trump is at heart a man of action.

Peace must be negotiated between Kiev, Brussels, Washington, and Moscow. The State of Israel must be allowed to finish the job of destroying Hamas. The Abraham Accords must be reinitiated. Beijing must be put on notice that a blockade or military quarantine of Taiwan is unacceptable. President Trump kept the peace before; now he must bring the world peace again.

Additionally, the United States adds $1 trillion to our national debt every one hundred days. President Trump will bring in Congress to hammer out a plan that stops America hurtling into a financial abyss while avoiding a major recession.

Last, President Trump will build the wall, seal the southern border, stop the invasion, and commence a firm yet humane program of mass deportations.

These actions are but the beginning of what must be done to save our country, to bequeath to future generations the Constitutional Republic that was bequeathed to us. A man of action is required, a man of destiny is required, a man whose fate is inextricably linked to the peace and prosperity of our Nation.

That man is Donald John Trump—and this book is about his thinking, policies, and actions.

In these chapters you have the lessons learned from the rock star of Trump's first term—and the foundation of those policies to come. It is exhilarating to read, energizing to think about. MAGA has now come of age. President Trump delivered not simply peace and prosperity in his first term—but he has given us a blueprint of how to continue to build upon it, taking America and the world to new heights.

Bravo, brother Navarro.

Introduction

As America's forty-fifth president, Donald John Trump provided the American people with unprecedented peace, prosperity, and national security. If elected on November 5, 2024, as America's forty-seventh president, he will do it again. This next time, however, it will be a much harder battle for Donald Trump and his advisers. Even as you read this book, far too many powerful special interests are massing to stop Trump!

Because of these special interests—from the corporate suites of America and Wall Street, to the K Street lobbyists of Big Pharma and the dark money of the vile Koch network—we are living in Joe Biden's America. This is a place where Joe Biden's stagflation is killing our economy, driving down the real wages of working-class America, and turning the retirement hopes and dreams of far too many Americans into an ash heap as 401(k)s are reduced to 201(k)s, cars are repossessed, and even once–middle-class Americans are being evicted from their homes.

Joe Biden's America is also a place where our southern border is being overrun; rogue nations from Communist China and Russia to Iran and North Korea are stoking the fires of war; Biden's FBI and Department of Justice have become weaponized partisan tools of the radical Left to punish and often imprison American citizens for their religious or political views; and the most commonsense political movement, Make America Great Again, has been turned into a four-letter word—MAGA—threatening to spark a civil war.

The wounds that Joe Biden is inflicting upon the American people will not be easily healed. Yet, if there is any one person capable of turning Joe Biden's America back into Trump's America, it is Donald Trump himself.

In this book, we will systematically work our way through many of the major problems facing this nation—our coverage is not exhaustive by design.

Most importantly, we will offer an action plan and set of policy prescriptions that a new Trump administration will likely begin to implement on *day one* of a new Trump presidency.

Ultimately, this book is much more than a book. It is a weapon of peaceful change in the hands of every Trump deplorable MAGA supporter. Only Donald Trump can return this great American nation back to the path of peace, prosperity, and national security, back to a world in which God, country, and family reign supreme.

As a final note before we get started, we would like to strongly reiterate the message of the subtitle of this guidebook: this is an *unofficial* guide to the Trump campaign.

While this guidebook draws heavily upon both the president's speeches and numerous policy postings on the Trump 2024 campaign website itself, only President Trump and his *official* spokespersons can be the final arbiters of the president's positions and campaign platform. With folks like Susie Wiles, Jason Miller, Chris LaCivita, Stephen Cheung, and Brian Jack assisting, the Trump 2024 campaign is in extremely good hands.

CHAPTER 1

The MAGA Messaging Imperative and Policy Agenda

In the November 2022 election, the Republican Party lost a golden opportunity to take back both the House of Representatives and the U.S. Senate when the vaunted Republican red wave most pundits had predicted never materialized. This failure was the result of four basic factors:

One: The Supreme Court's overturning of *Roe v. Wade* and a concomitant political backlash that boosted Democrat turnout.

Two: The internecine warfare within the Republican Party, pitting corporate and Wall Street– backed traditional never-Trump RINO Republicans against the Populist Economic Nationalism of Donald Trump, which resulted in highly damaging attack ads on MAGA Republican candidates paid for by Republican leadership in both the Senate and House.

Three: A superior Democrat electoral strategy that focused on stuffing as many Democrat votes into the ballot box in the weeks and months preceding election day versus a Republican "game day" strategy that relied on heavy turnout on election day subject to strategic gaming by the Democrats.

Four: The Bidenites' profane turning of the political slogan of MAGA—Make America Great Again—from a noble, blue-collar badge emblemizing God, country, family, and the dignity of work to that of a slogan synonymous with extremism and domestic terrorism.

To win in 2024, the Republican Party must squarely address each of the first three of these factors. Yet, if Donald Trump is ultimately to be successful in the 2024 election, it is critical that the broad electorate understands exactly what MAGA truly represents.

It was Ronald Reagan, in his 1980 acceptance speech at the Republican National Convention in Detroit, who gave birth to the modern MAGA movement. Said Reagan:

> *For those without skills, we'll find a way to help them get skills. For those without job opportunities, we'll stimulate new opportunities, particularly in the inner cities where they live. For those who have abandoned hope, we'll restore hope and we'll welcome them into a great national crusade to make America great again!*

Reagan also had this to say, which cuts to the core of the work I did at the White House on behalf of Donald Trump:

> *Work and family are at the center of our lives; the foundation of our dignity as a free people. When we deprive people of*

what they have earned, or take away their jobs, we destroy their dignity and undermine their families. We cannot support our families unless there are jobs; and we cannot have jobs unless people have both money to invest and the faith to invest it.

During the November 2022 election campaign, Joe Biden turned the beauty of this MAGA poetry into a four-letter word. In his infamous "Red Wedding" blood-red background speech on September 1, 2022, Biden falsely equated those associated with Trump's MAGA with violence and extremism, calling MAGA Republicans a "clear and present danger" to our democracy.

Biden also sought to divide and conquer the Republican Party with these words:

Not every Republican, not even the majority of Republicans, are MAGA Republicans. Not every Republican embraces their extreme ideology.

Democrats, independents, mainstream Republicans: We must be stronger, more determined, and more committed to saving American democracy than MAGA Republicans are—to destroying American democracy.

Just six days later, a Reuters/Ipsos poll reported that 58 percent of respondents, including one in four Republicans, said Trump's Make America Great Again movement is threatening America's democratic foundations.

Today, Biden's profane assault on MAGA represents a cornerstone of the Democrats' presidential attack strategy. If Donald Trump is to succeed in the 2024 election where the Republican Party failed in 2022, the American people must gain a much better understanding of what MAGA means and what the modern MAGA movement stands for.

Perhaps the best and simplest way to describe the meaning of MAGA—and the essence of Trumpism—is through an iron triangle of Populist Economic Nationalism. The first leg of this iron MAGA triangle is to *strengthen America's manufacturing and defense industrial base.*

Such strengthening can be done through policies like hefty tariffs on Communist China and strict adherence to Buy American, Hire American government procurement policies. The broader *economic* goal is to provide good-paying jobs for America's working-class and middle-income families.

The equally important *national security* goal is to bring our supply chains home and thereby make them more resilient and less vulnerable to attack or the economic blackmail of foreign manufacturers like Communist China.

The second leg of the Populist Economic Nationalist MAGA triangle is that of *secure borders.* During the Trump administration, this meant, first and foremost, building a smart and impregnable wall on our border with Mexico. Does the chant "Build that wall! Build that wall!" ring a bell?

Here are some key facts worth noting: Historically, more than 90 percent of illegal aliens crossing our southern border have come from Mexico and the three countries of the so-called Northern Triangle—Guatemala, El Salvador, and Honduras. More than 50 percent of these illegal aliens have less than an eighth-grade education and only 25 percent are proficient in the English language.

It follows that many of these poorly educated, English-illiterate, illegal aliens will compete against America's poor and blue-collar working classes. The inevitable results are fewer job opportunities and lower wages for working-class Americans.

America's low-income Blacks and Hispanics don't need PhDs in economics to understand these labor market pressures. At a visceral level, they understand that open borders are bad for them and secure borders will improve their lives.

It's not for nothing that in the 2020 election, Donald Trump significantly outperformed his 2016 vote totals in both the Black and Hispanic communities. This was a pure MAGA Populist Economic Nationalist response and it can happen again in 2024.

The third leg of the iron MAGA triangle is *an end to America's endless wars*. These wars are waged sometimes covertly and sometimes out in the shock-and-awe open.

They are wars fought in far-off hell holes that stretch from the Hindu Kush of Afghanistan and gunboat-infested waters of the Persian Gulf to the deserts of Iraq and the Horn of Africa. Mostly, they are wars that have been fought for so long that many Americans—particularly the elites far from the battle lines—have forgotten why these wars were started to begin with.

From the MAGA point of view, these endless wars are propagated by RINO warmongers like Bush and Cheney. They are perpetuated by weaklings trying to look strong like Obama and Biden.

These endless wars are not moral and necessary wars like World War I and World War II. Rather, they are futile and pernicious "plowshares into swords" wars that have drained trillions of dollars from the American economy to the benefit of a military-industrial complex, at the expense of modernizing our infrastructure, improving our schools, and lowering our taxes. Just imagine what America would be like right now if that blood had not been spilled and those trillions of dollars of American treasure had not been squandered.

Taken together, these three legs of the Populist Economic Nationalist triangle—a rebirth of American manufacturing, stemming the tide of illegal immigration, and halting our endless wars—almost perfectly define the Trump deplorable base. It's a different kind of Rainbow Coalition base that brings together working-class Americans of all colors who seek a good job at a decent wage and an end to being sacrificial lambs in America's globalist offshoring ventures and foreign war adventures.

If we are to win back the White House and take total control of Congress in 2024, it is critical, however, that the American people also understand clearly that MAGA is the antithesis of a four-letter word. In Trump's America, MAGA is about God, country, and family. The way those of us in the MAGA community believe we can live in peace and prosperity is by building a strong American manufacturing and defense industrial base, securing our borders, and putting an end to endless wars.

This is who we are; and we should not let the Democrats and the corporate media take this, our very identity, away from us.

You, as a MAGA ambassador in your community, must explain to your family and friends and associates what MAGA means and what we in MAGA stand for—and against. Put most simply:

- There is no path to a Trump victory if MAGA remains tarred with the Biden brush of "extremism."

- The first and most important campaign mission is to clearly articulate what MAGA represents.
- Every Trump supporter in America must become a MAGA ambassador capable of clearly articulating the MAGA iron triangle of Populist Economic Nationalism and how we seek only peace, prosperity, and national security.

CHAPTER 2

=======

The ACTION, ACTION, ACTION Plan
to Take Back Trump's America

Before we talk about each of the *big* policy issues Donald Trump must address for the American people, it is important to talk about the broad policy approach the coming Trump White House will embrace. Once Donald Trump takes back control of the White House, he will begin acting on Inauguration Day.

As Steve Bannon used to say during my White House years, the organizational culture of the Trump White House is embodied in this canon: "Action, Action, Action."

During my four years serving as one of President Trump's most loyal and trusted advisers, I learned firsthand that the most powerful policy tool any president wields is the ability to issue presidential executive orders and presidential memoranda. If crafted properly, such "EOs" and "PMs," as they are called, offer the fastest path to policy reforms.

By way of background here, I was involved in the drafting and signing of more than thirty such instruments during my tenure in the West Wing—and there is good reason for that. The sad reality here is that legislation often moves at a glacial pace and during the Trump administration, even when Republicans controlled *both* the House of Representatives and the Senate, there were too many Republicans in Name Only (RINO) to get Trump actions into law. (Senate Majority Leader Mitch McConnell and, before he left, House Speaker Paul Ryan were bitter Never-Trump pills we were constantly forced to swallow.)

Of course, the big downside to a sole reliance on executive orders and presidential memoranda is the ability of a successor president to undo them with the stroke of a pen. This, in fact, is precisely what Joe Biden did with many of Trump's actions during his first term—always with disastrous results.

For example, as you will see in this book, Biden's repeal of President Trump's "safe third nation" agreements with Mexico and the Northern Triangle countries of El Salvador, Guatemala, and Honduras turned America's southern border from a secure one to a dangerously open one.

Hitting close to my "home" in the Trump administration, the Bidenites also canceled a number of the Buy American, Hire American executive orders I helped craft. Not surprisingly, our trade deficit continues to soar and our supply chains continue to suffer from overreliance on unreliable and competitor countries.

Because executive actions are so easy to undo, the Trump administration will, as part of the action plan, also seek to memorialize each executive action into legislation. This is a quite workable strategy if (but only if) Trump Republicans gain control of both the House and Senate.

In each remaining chapter of this book, various members of the team who contributed to this work will lay out a specific issue to be addressed and then offer the set of solutions that will be implemented first by executive action and then, where applicable, by follow-up legislation.

A key element of these solutions will be the Trump principle that "economic security is national security." For example, if we lose our factories to Communist China because of unfair trade, we don't just lose good jobs at good wages. America loses the productive capacity it needs to defend itself.

Remember the automobile and aircraft factories of America were transformed into an arsenal of democracy in World War II.

President Trump's dictum that economic security equals national security is an important principle because much of the legal authority underlying the presidential actions President Trump will take is rooted in the national security imperative.

With that said, and as my old boss used to say: "Let's go!"

CHAPTER 3

The Buy American,
Hire American Imperative

During his first term, President Trump governed by two simple rules: Buy American and Hire American. This quintessential Make America Great (and Prosperous) Again policy was implemented through numerous executive orders that directly or indirectly strengthened the U.S. government's Buy American procurement policies, expanding coverage, tightening enforcement, and eliminating waivers.

During *his* first term, Joe Biden is using more and more American taxpayer dollars to strengthen the manufacturing and defense industrial base of Communist China, a country that poses the greatest existential threat to America in our history. Clearly, with the 2024 election, we must elect Donald Trump and go back to his Buy American future.

Each year, more than thirty federal agencies award close to $1 trillion in federal financial assistance to more than forty thousand nonfederal recipient organizations. By ensuring these federal agencies rely on both American products and workers, our nation's Buy American programs create high-paying manufacturing jobs and thereby help lift more and more of America's blue-collar workers into middle-class prosperity.

In addition, about twenty cents on every dollar spent on Buy American comes back to the government in the form of taxes paid by corporations earning profits on Buy American projects, workers earning wages on these projects, and states deriving more sales tax revenues.

From a national security point of view, Buy American spending also strengthens our manufacturing and defense industrial base, including pillar industries like steel and aluminum that are so vital to defense weapons production and national security.

Joe Biden has turned all of this on its head. His massive Green New Deal infrastructure overspending bills have not only helped fuel demand-pull inflation, but they are also helping to offshore many of our factories and supply chains, principally to Communist China.

Consider, for example, Biden's solar tax credits. Biden not only continues to allow Communist China to dump unfairly subsidized solar panels into the U.S. market and thereby suppress U.S. productive capacity, but he is also forcing U.S. taxpayers to pay for the importation of Made in China silicon wafers used in the assembly of panels on U.S. soil.

Consider, too, the Biden regime's heavy push and taxpayer shove for electric vehicles. Strip away the Biden woke green agenda rhetoric, Biden's EV tax credits represent the Full Employment Act for Red Chinese parts manufacturers, particularly high value-added parts such as lithium batteries. These tax credits are also deeply regressive, going primarily to the highest-income households.

In a related Biden fiasco, a woke Pentagon leadership now focused more on green, gender, and diversity ideologies than combat readiness is pushing for an all-electric, non-tactical vehicle fleet by 2030. In Biden's military, our vehicles will be powered by Communist batteries made in Chinese factories—this is a United States military, by the way, that is already far too dependent on foreign imports, including the integrated circuits used in cell phones, cruise missiles, drones, and satellites.

While much of the focus of President Trump's Buy American policies early in his first term targeted traditional manufacturing like steel and aluminum, the Communist Chinese–manufactured pandemic has both revealed and underscored the need for thinking about Buy American and the need to bring *both* our factories and supply chains home in a much broader contract.

As one of the authors of this book (Peter Navarro) would learn firsthand as the president's Defense Production Act Policy coordinator, the darkest days of the pandemic revealed critical manufacturing and supply-chain shortages for everything from the personal protective equipment we needed to defend ourselves to the medicines and vitamins necessary to prevent and fight infection. And yes, at one critical point, Communist China threatened to drown the American devils in a "sea of coronavirus" if we dared accuse them of doing exactly what they had done—unleash the deadly COVID-19 virus from a Wuhan lab.

In a post-pandemic world, we also have come to realize the *economic* dangers of relying on far-flung supply chains globally dispersed around the world. Here, a lack of global supply chain resilience and concomitant shortages in products ranging from food and beverages to key pharmaceuticals and even Christmas decorations have contributed significantly to inflation—almost three-quarters of the forty most popular brand-name drugs are imported.

In light of this strategic chess board, President Trump will double and triple down on the need for the enforcement of Buy American policies. To further promote such policies, he will issue executive orders and take all other necessary actions to

- Further expand coverage and enforcement of Buy American policies, particularly to industries critical to national security.
- Ensure that no taxpayer monies are used to finance the foreign production of manufactured products, particularly in Communist China.

CHAPTER 4

An America First Budget Will Turn Us Back from the Fiscal Cliff

by Russ Vought, former director of the Office of Management and Budget

The United States continues to face fiscal peril. The country now owes $33 trillion and counting, and the interest on the debt is steadily marching higher and higher, crowding out legitimate government priorities. The annual cost of interest payments will exceed the Pentagon's budget within the next ten years, and already Americans are experiencing forty-year highs in inflation.

The Left has no interest in regaining fiscal rationality and their priorities and institutions should be radically defunded. They are not just unaffordable; they are actively destroying the country.

For decades, our policymakers have squandered each and every opportunity to control spending by their unwillingness to develop a reform agenda that speaks to the priorities of the American people. That must change, and thankfully a template is provided by the balanced budgets that President Trump sent to Congress each year that were repeatedly ignored to keep spending at high levels.

A balanced budget within ten years can be achieved through a combination of robust economic growth and sizable spending reductions. Both are vital.

You cannot cut your way to balance in a slowly growing economy. The target balance will keep getting bigger as revenues dry up, while the public experiences the pain of unemployment and austerity at the same time.

Nor can you balance the budget through more robust growth alone. Economic growth of 3 percent—achievable under Trump policies, impossible under Bidenomics—and roughly $9 trillion in savings and spending cuts and reforms is required.

On the growth side, the types of policies that will generate this kind of growth are making permanent the Trump-era tax cuts (TCJA), providing full expensing of all capital assets and renewing deregulatory efforts and aggressive energy exploration. On spending, nearly a third of the savings should come from discretionary spending, primarily dismantling the woke and weaponized bureaucracy. The rest must be generated from reforms to mandatory spending that increase participation in the labor force and reduce welfare. No reductions to Social Security retirement or Medicare benefits are needed.

Most critically, we must defund the hundreds of billions now being spent each year to fuel a federal bureaucracy that is both woke and weaponized against much of the country. This bureaucracy furthers a woke agenda that divides Americans through grants, contracts, and regulatory decisions.

On the woke front, the Department of Education is not interested in teacher improvement and student test scores, but in pushing Critical Race Theory aimed at fomenting cultural revolution through our schools. HUD is not interested in ending homelessness, but rather in spreading crime and dysfunction into safe neighborhoods under the guise of "fair housing" activism. The State Department is no longer simply wasting money through foreign aid on items like a Bob Dylan statue in Mozambique or a NASA space camp in Pakistan. It, too, is pushing a woke agenda in countries that oppose it, whether it's funding a gay pride parade in Prague or LGBT activists in Senegal.

On the weaponized bureaucracy front, the FBI is not interested in traditional law enforcement but rather investigating concerned parents for "domestic terrorism," sending SWAT teams to arrest pro-life activists and conducting raids on former President Trump and his closest advisers. The EPA even put a seventy-seven-year-old U.S. Navy veteran in jail for eighteen months for building ponds on his ranch to fight wildfires.

This wasting of taxpayer billions on woke and weaponized partisan agendas must be stopped in its tracks if America is to return to its roots of self-government.

There are also dramatic savings to be harvested from reforming so-called "mandatory" spending. By scaling back an overly generous welfare system, we can help boost labor force participation rates and stimulate economic growth.

Such reforms include returning Medicaid to a program focused on vulnerable populations instead of able-bodied working-age individuals, adding a work requirement to the food stamp program to encourage individuals to get back into the workforce, lowering the cost of prescription drugs, focusing disability insurance on the actually disabled instead of those who can get different jobs in the economy, and ensuring that illegal immigrants cannot qualify for various tax credits, which continues to be the status quo. These policy changes will generate significant savings over ten years.

Budgeting is too often an exercise in accounting and austerity, where every program takes a hit, rather than an opportunity to examine what in fact the country is spending money on. It is no surprise that such budgets have failed. By sharp contrast, President Trump's America First budget will achieve the necessary fiscal rebalancing while still providing the resources for national needs, such as adequately funding our defenses to confront adversaries such as Communist China, extending the border wall and securing the border, and rebuilding the country's deteriorating infrastructure.

Time is of the essence. The fiscal picture is only getting worse. Only an America First budget dealing sufficiently with our nation's fiscal recklessness *and* aimed at the most serious policy threats facing our country offers a realistic chance out of the cul-de-sac of fiscal inaction that Americans have come to know.

CHAPTER 5

President Trump Will Unwind the Follies of Bidenomics

America's looming fiscal cliff is as unprecedented as it is staggering. The clear culprit is Joe Biden's half-baked, harebrained economics.

The legislation that most defines Bidenomics—the American Rescue Plan, the Infrastructure Investment and Jobs Act, and the (anything but) Inflation Reduction Act—are catalyzing the most rapid increase in America's national debt ever witnessed in a peacetime economy.

According to the Congressional Budget Office, America's debt will soar from $33 trillion today to $45 trillion in 2030. By 2050, the annual federal budget deficit will increase from 5 percent of GDP in 2030 to a mind-bending 13 percent.

In the short run, the U.S. Treasury is selling trillions of dollars in bonds at ever-higher interest rates to finance the Bidenomics debt. This borrowing surge is putting unrelenting upward pressure on interest rates, mortgage rates, and credit card rates, and it is already beginning to choke off economic growth.

In the long run, the U.S. government will devote more and more of its tax revenues just to service the Bidenomics debt. This debt service will come at the expense of funding everything from roads, bridges, and national defense to Medicare and Social Security, even as it transfers American wealth to foreign bondholders.

Absent significant cutbacks in future spending baked into the U.S. budget by Bidenomics, the U.S. government has two ways to address its growing debt problem. It can raise taxes, as Democrats are now pressing for. However, such a contractionary fiscal policy would further slow economic growth and likely reduce net revenues.

Alternatively, the U.S. Treasury, in cooperation with the Federal Reserve, can simply print new money to pay off the debt. However, this strategy, known as "monetizing the debt," comes at an even greater cost: more inflation and possibly hyperinflation.

Faced with such a Hobson's choice, Congress's third—and really "first best"—solution is to dramatically claw back significant chunks of future spending dictated in the Bidenomics budget. President Trump will lead this charge, starting with an elimination of all the electric vehicle mandates and subsidies.

The fiscal apocalypse we are facing is no run-of-the-mill, banana republic, Argentina-style meltdown easily resolved by an international default on U.S. debt and a simple debt restructuring. Rather, it's a 1970s-style stagflation on steroids.

Bidenomics initially lit the inflation portion of the stagflation candle with a series of massive Keynesian overstimuli. The resultant price shocks have since been exacerbated by energy and food price shocks.

These energy and food price shocks are largely the result of Joe Biden's war on American oil producers and bungling of Russia's invasion of Ukraine, coupled with Biden's ceding of the leadership of the oil cartel OPEC to the world's two biggest oil producers besides the United States—Saudi Arabia and Russia. Thanks to Biden's fecklessness, Saudi princes and Vladimir Putin now set oil prices, not the United States; energy prices are now more than 50 percent higher than during the Trump years and climbing still.

Biden's inflation has, in turn, provoked the Federal Reserve into its fastest rate hikes in more than thirty years. The resultant credit crunch is now squeezing key sectors of the economy, choking economic growth and bringing into play the "stag," or stagnation, part of the stagflation equation.

Absent a fiscally responsible debt limit deal, Main Street will feel the pain for years to come in the form of higher unemployment and depressed real wages. Meanwhile, slowing economic growth and increased financing costs are already reverberating up and down Wall Street—with a severe market correction a growing likelihood in the short run and more meager rates of return on stock market investing over the longer run.

Of course, none of this would be happening under a Trump administration. Once again, as with America's humiliation in Afghanistan, capitulation to Communist China, and invasion at our southern border, Joe Biden teaches us in the hardest of ways that elections have consequences. Let us all pray now for the victory of Donald John Trump over the folly of Bidenomics.

CHAPTER 6

Defending American Jobs Through Fair, Balanced, and Reciprocal Trade

During the Biden regime, the overall U.S. trade deficit, including goods and services, has soared to more than a trillion dollars annually. This Biden monstrosity implicitly measures the large amounts of America's manufacturing, defense industrial base, and supply chains that have been offshored to foreign lands.

Such offshoring suppresses the real wages of American blue-collar workers and denies millions of Americans the opportunity to climb up the rungs of the ladder to the middle class. It raises the specter of a manufacturing and defense industrial base that, unlike in World Wars I and II, will not be able to provide the weapons and material needed should America enter another major world war—or seek to assist a major ally like Europe, Japan, or Taiwan.

Remember here the admonition of Russia's Josef Stalin that

"quantity has a quality of its own." During World War II, it was not just the brave soldiers, sailors, and pilots who beat the Nazis and Imperial Japan. It was America's factories—its "arsenal of democracy"—that overwhelmed the Axis forces.

Add all this up, and America's trade situation and its massive trade imbalances pose a severe economic security threat. As President Donald Trump indicated in announcing his 2017 National Security Strategy, "Economic security *is* national security."

A root cause of America's chronic trade deficit is that there is a set of unfair and nonreciprocal international trading rules that, as administered by the World Trade Organization (WTO), are driving America's factories offshore and flooding U.S. markets with heavily subsidized imports.

Under the WTO's "most favored nation" (MFN) rule, each WTO member must apply the lowest tariffs it applies to the products of any *one* country to the products of *every other* WTO country.

Importantly, *nothing* in the MFN rule requires a WTO member to provide equal—that is, *reciprocal* or *mirror*—tariff rates to its trading partners. Rather, under MFN, WTO members can charge systematically higher tariffs to other countries to the extent negotiated in their WTO tariff schedules as long as they apply those same higher tariffs to all countries.

As a poster child for the kind of nonreciprocal tariffs American manufacturers often face, the MFN tariff for autos applied by the United States is only 2.5 percent. In contrast, the EU charges 10 percent on the imports of U.S. autos, Communist China levies 15 percent, and Brazil 35 percent.

Similarly, while the United States applies an MFN tariff rate of 6.2 percent on the rice it buys from Malaysia, Malaysia applies an ad-valorem equivalent tariff of 40 percent on rice from the United States. Meanwhile, European milk producers are shielded by 67 percent tariffs, while American milk producers benefit from only a 15 percent tariff on foreign imports.

From the perspective of strategic game theory, the WTO's MFN rule provides little or no incentive for higher tariff countries to lower their tariffs. Rather, under these conditions, the *dominant strategy* of any relatively high tariff country is simply to maintain those high tariffs while free-riding off the lower tariff countries. Of course, those countries hurt most by the WTO's nonreciprocal tariff regime are those like the United States that charge the lowest tariffs on average.

Note here that Communist China levies higher tariffs on *ten* products for every *one* product the United States applies higher tariffs on Communist China. India's ratio is even higher at *thirteen* to one.

Further, both Communist China and India also feature significant nontariff barriers. Collectively, these higher nonreciprocal tariffs in Communist China and India block American exporters from selling goods at competitive prices to more than one-third of the world's population.

Under current United States laws and regulations, an American president has limited ability to fight back against the higher MFN tariffs now being levied against American workers, farmers, ranchers, and manufacturers. Accordingly, behind the protective WTO shield of MFN, America's free-riding trading partners have little or no incentive to come to the bargaining table to negotiate lower tariffs and provide American manufacturers and workers with a far more level playing field.

To address this nonreciprocity stalemate, President Donald J. Trump urged Congress in his 2019 State of the Union address to pass the U.S. Reciprocal Trade Act (USRTA). The USRTA would provide the president with the authority to bring any American trading partner currently applying higher nonreciprocal tariffs to the negotiating table. If that trading partner refuses to lower tariffs to U.S. levels, the president then has the authority to raise U.S. tariffs to match or "mirror" the foreign partner's tariffs.

The USRTA bill was introduced on January 24, 2019, by Representative Sean Duffy (R-WI). The following month, a Harvard-Harris poll of 1,792 registered voters found that 80 percent of respondents supported the USRTA. As Representative Duffy noted at the time, the purpose of granting the president these authorities was *not* to raise tariffs. Rather, it was to provide the president, working in close consultation with Congress, a sophisticated and targeted tool to force other countries to lower their tariffs and nontariff barriers.

According to an analysis conducted by my office within the Trump White House, the Office of Trade and Manufacturing Policy, if all 132 countries were to lower their higher nonreciprocal tariffs to U.S. levels, this would reduce the overall U.S. trade deficit in goods by almost 10 percent.

In contrast, if these countries were to refuse to reciprocate and the United States were to raise its tariffs to mirror those countries' levels, the reduction in the U.S. trade deficit would be of a similar magnitude.

Either way, far more fair, reciprocal, and balanced trade under the USRTA would create hundreds of thousands of new jobs while strengthening our manufacturing and defense industrial base.

President Trump is committed to passage of the USRTA in his second term. He will also crack down unmercifully on the trade cheaters and continue to negotiate and renegotiate trade deals to the advantage of the American nation.

CHAPTER 7

Decoupling the U.S. Economy from a Cheating Communist China

Of all its bilateral trade relationships, America's relationship with Communist China is the most fraught. The problem is not just Communist China's relentless mercantilist and protectionist *trade policies* following its accession to the WTO in 2001, which have led to chronic, massive, and ever-expanding trade deficits.

Communist China's economic aggression is further facilitated by equally aggressive Chinese *industrial policies* designed to shift the manufacturing and supply chains of the world to Communist Chinese soil. Of course, the Chinese Communist Party's (CCP) broader goal is to strengthen Communist China's defense industrial base and associated warfighting capabilities.

That the CCP unabashedly seeks to supplant America as the world's dominant economic and military power is not in dispute.

Rather, it is a prominent feature of the rhetoric of Xi Jinping, the dictator of Communist China. By 2049, the one-hundred-year anniversary of the Chinese Communist nation, Xi has promised the deed will be done.

President Trump understood this existential threat better than anyone who ever inhabited the Oval Office. That the CCP and Xi Jinping have no intention of ever honoring any trade agreement with the United States or of ceasing Communist China's relentless mercantilist attack is beyond dispute.

Upon taking office in 2017, President Trump put on hold his 2016 campaign promise to immediately put high tariffs on Chinese products. Instead, as a gesture of good faith, he sought to negotiate a comprehensive trade agreement that would eliminate Communist China's unfair trade practices.

By the middle of 2018, it was clear the CCP had no intention of bargaining in good faith. On June 15, President Trump began levying tariffs that would eventually rise to cover more than $500 billion of Chinese imports.

In April 2019, these tariffs would lead Communist China's lead negotiator, Vice Premier Liu He, to tentatively agree to what would have been the most comprehensive trade deal in global history. Yet, on May 3, 2019, Liu would renege on that 150-page deal and seek to drastically retrade it.

The result was derisively called a "skinny deal" that has been a predictable bust as Communist China failed to both consummate a significant fraction of its promised purchases of U.S. products and has made no progress on reforming its mercantilist, protectionist, and technology transfer-forcing policies.

What Donald Trump has learned from that is that the Chinese

Communist Party cannot be trusted to honor any agreement it might enter into, and the only way to fight the CCP's legendary cheating and mercantilist assault is to *completely decouple the U.S. economy from China.*

The case for decoupling begins in China's "Seven Deadly Mercantilist Sins." These include intellectual property theft, counterfeiting and piracy, forced technology transfer by American companies to China as a condition of market entry, the massive dumping of products below cost into American markets, heavily subsidized state-owned enterprises that unfairly compete, and currency manipulation.

As a seventh sin, Communist China has engineered a deadly assault on America's children and workers through its export of deadly fentanyl. This lethal opioid disproportionately kills otherwise healthy Americans in our blue-collar manufacturing force and thereby attacks our defense industrial base.

Not surprisingly, Joe Biden, who is deeply compromised both directly and indirectly through his criminal son Hunter, has done nothing to pressure the Chinese dictator Xi Jinping and the CCP to stop their "Seven Deadly Sins" assault. If we are to save our country, America has no other choice than to decouple.

Decoupling from Communist China's economy must be done strategically and smartly. In far too many areas, the United States is far too dependent on China. Where such dependencies exist, we must move more slowly, even as we move more rapidly to develop indigenous supply chains and production to address these dependencies.

The primary tool President Trump can use—and will use—to decouple from Communist China is the Trump tariffs. Besides protecting the American factories and American workers from

China's mercantilist assault, these tariffs will also help dramatically reduce America's massive trade deficit.

Communist China accounts for almost 40 percent of America's more than $1 trillion trade deficit; and to be clear here, trade deficits do indeed matter. They both dramatically reduce our economic growth and transfer American wealth in the form of both dollars and assets like land and companies to Communist China.

In his second term, President Trump should

- Strategically expand tariffs to all foreign and especially Chinese-made products utilizing a universal baseline tariff, and ramp tariff rates up to levels that will block out Made in China products; execute this strategy in a manner and at a pace that will not expose the United States to a lack of access to essential products, like key pharmaceuticals.
- Provide significant financial and tax incentives to American companies seeking onshore production from Communist China to U.S. soil.
- Stop Communist China's abuse of the so-called "de minimis exemption," which allows Communist China to evade tariffs for products less than $800.
- Prohibit Communist Chinese state-owned enterprises from bidding on U.S. government procurement contracts, such as those for subway and other transportation systems.
- Systematically reduce and eventually eliminate any U.S. dependence on Communist Chinese supply chains that may be used to threaten national security—medicines, silicon chips, rare earth minerals, computer motherboards, flatscreen displays, and military components.

- Reinvigorate and expand the Department of Homeland Security crackdown initiated by the Trump administration on the CCP's use of e-sellers, such as Amazon, eBay, and Alibaba, to flood U.S. markets with counterfeit and pirated goods.

America gets fleeced every day in the global marketplace by a predatory Communist China. Joe Biden and the Democrats have further enabled the Communist Chinese. Donald Trump will stop Communist China and its cheaters in their tracks.

CHAPTER 8

America's Pension Funds and IRAs Must Stop Funding the Chinese Military

by Frank J. Gaffney, founder and president of the Center for Security Policy

The Chinese Communist Party is, bar none, the most dangerous enemy the United States has ever faced and the greatest existential threat to freedom in world history. It is, therefore, absolutely insane that the U.S. financial sector continues to enable Communist China's rapid militarization by underwriting it with the pensions and other savings of tens of millions of unwitting Americans.

This formula for our destruction is one of the most egregious byproducts of the CCP's determined "elite capture" of our leading financiers. Individuals like Larry Fink of BlackRock, Stephen Schwarzman of Blackstone Group, Bridgewater founder Ray Dalio, Jamie Dimon at J.P. Morgan Chase, and their counterparts at firms like Vanguard, MSCI, FTSE Russell, Goldman Sachs, and

State Street have been enormously enriched in the course of their dealings with the Chinese Communists.

In exchange, such self-styled "masters of the universe" have, over time, not only sluiced trillions of U.S. investor dollars into Chinese Communist coffers via the abuse of our capital markets. As a top Communist Chinese Party influence operator, Dr. Di Dongsheng gloated in December 2020 that China's "old friends" on Wall Street have also been—with the exception of the Trump years—hugely helpful as lobbyists for the PRC in Washington.

Huge donations from the financial sector have helped ensure that successive administrations and Congresses of both parties have kept America's pension fund money flowing to corporations controlled by and enabling the Chinese Communist Party. Even more outrageous, some of those companies are *directly* aiding the People's Liberation Army's massive and increasingly ominous buildup.

During his first term, President Trump certainly understood the danger of both infusions of capital into China and the influence exercised by those *literally* in its pocket in the U.S. capital markets. Yet many of President Trump's initiatives—including efforts to delist or otherwise sanction Chinese Communist companies on the New York Stock Exchange or NASDAQ—were thwarted by the Communist Chinese collaborators *in the Trump administration*, most notably Treasury Secretary Steven Mnuchin and SEC chairman Jay Clayton.

Of particular note is President Trump's 2020 decision to block Communist Chinese access to the $750 *billion* worth of pension savings of U.S. government civilian and military employees that are managed by the federal Thrift Savings Plan (TSP). In principle, this blockade would be applied to all Communist Chinese investment. As National Security Advisor Robert O'Brien warned:

> *It has come to our attention that billions of dollars from our federal employees' retirement fund will soon be invested in Chinese companies. This action would expose the retirement fund to significant and unnecessary risk. And it would channel money from federal employees' money to companies that present significant national security and humanitarian concerns.*

In practice, however, many Chinese companies are still allowed to draw on U.S. pension fund dollars because they are based in Hong Kong rather than the Chinese mainland. Indeed, today, all current military and civilian federal employees and many retirees who chose a diversified portfolio, including investments in the I Fund of the Thrift Savings Plan, are obliged to put their money into Communist China.

On top of this, in 2022, the Thrift Savings Plan opened a so-called mutual fund window. It offered TSP participants the opportunity to invest a portion of their savings in one or more of some five thousand mutual funds *without identifying which held Chinese companies.* In fact, some twenty-two of these funds are composed of *only* Chinese companies.

At a time when Communist China's dictator Xi Jinping is preparing his nation for a shooting war against not just Taiwan *but America*, the United States must cease the transfer of wealth from American pension funds and other investment vehicles that are paying for such preparations, among other malevolent activities, and President Trump will do just that.

A further reality must be a decisive consideration: American investments will surely be lost altogether in the event of a conflict with Communist China. This will add material financial insult to the mortal injury likely to be thus inflicted.

These are the executive actions available to a new Trump presidency. Expect quick and decisive action.

- The Thrift Savings Plan should remove from its International Fund all Chinese companies and from its mutual fund window offerings that hold Chinese corporate securities.
- It should be illegal for American retailers and institutions to hold the securities (read: stocks and bonds) of Communist Chinese companies doing business with, or otherwise directly or indirectly supporting, the People's Liberation Army.
- Those Chinese companies listed on U.S. capital markets should be delisted and deregistered.
- All American mutual funds, exchange-traded funds, and other passive investment vehicles that are held in the portfolios of Chinese "A Share" companies should be divested immediately and barred from further American investment.
- The issuance of dollar-denominated Chinese sovereign bonds should be made illegal.
- Any Chinese companies sanctioned by the United States in any way should be barred from U.S. capital markets and made off-limits to private equity investors.
- Variable interest entities as listing vehicles for Chinese companies on American exchanges out of the Cayman Islands and elsewhere offshore should be made illegal.

CHAPTER 9

A Bidenomics March to Strategic
Energy Subservience

In four short years, Green New Dealer-in-Chief Joe Biden has turned America's strategic energy dominance into a strategic energy subservience that gravely threatens our economic and national security. We now run the very real risks of prolonged stagflation and being drawn into hot wars from anywhere between Ukraine, Israel, and Iran to the Taiwan Strait.

During Donald Trump's first term as president, he accomplished the seemingly impossible. He turned the United States into the world's largest petroleum producer and a net exporter.

Once strategically energy-dominant, America became the de facto policeman of the OPEC oil cartel and world price-setter. If OPEC tried to gouge us by restricting supply, America could further increase production. That leverage, coupled with President

Trump's jawboning of the Saudis, kept oil prices substantially below what they have been throughout the Biden regime.

From day one, Joe Biden declared war on fossil fuels. He canceled pipelines, curtailed drilling, discouraged fracking, and turned this nation into the oil supplicant that it is today.

Now, it is Saudi Arabia and Russia—the world's two largest oil producers outside the United States—setting world oil prices. Saudi princes need at least $85 per barrel to fund the government programs the kingdom uses to pacify an increasingly restive population. Putin's Russia needs at least $100 per barrel to fund its Ukrainian adventure.

The resultant oil price shocks have been highly inflationary. Such higher oil prices act as a tax on consumers and thereby reduce purchasing power, with collateral negative demand effects. As we saw in the 1970s, higher oil prices likewise increased the cost of production and transportation for businesses and thereby reduced output through negative supply effects. Together, these negative growth effects represent the "stag" part of the oil price shock stagflation equation.

Normally, the Federal Reserve can treat such oil price shocks as transitory, which is to say cyclical, and leave them out of the core inflation metric the Fed relies upon to set short-term interest rates. If, however, higher oil prices represent a secular, long-term trend because of a Bidenomics-driven tectonic shift, sustained oil price hikes have to be factored into the Fed's calculus. That will surely mean higher interest rates for a far more extended period.

These economic risks pale in comparison to the national security risks from America's increasing oil import dependence and strategic energy subservience. Consider, first, Russia.

Even as American taxpayers are funding the Ukrainian war

effort to the tune of tens of billions of dollars (while draining the American arsenal), American consumers and businesses, through a pure wealth transfer, are funding the Russian war machine as more and more Russian oil creeps into world markets. The more oil revenue Russia captures, the less likely there will be peace, and the more likely the United States will be dragged into a hot war on the European continent.

A Joe Biden desperate for cheaper oil has similarly relaxed sanctions on the sale of Iranian oil. Iranian oil production has climbed from about 2.7 million barrels a day at the end of the Trump administration to almost 3.5 million today.

With the price of oil now bouncing between $80 and $90, that's an additional $2 billion a month Iran has to both keep its regime afloat and finance attacks on Israel and Saudi Arabia through proxies like Hezbollah, Hamas, the Houthi movement, Muslim Brotherhood, and Al-Mukhtar Brigades.

There is also the new Cuba in our South American midst, in Venezuela. It, too, is now being allowed by the Biden regime to increase its oil production, sell its oil in international markets to keep its toxic regime afloat, and export both its socialism to the rest of Latin America and its illegal aliens to American cities. What can go wrong there?

Finally, as a rising Communist China eyes an invasion of Taiwan after successfully taking Hong Kong, its dictator Xi Jinping has leveraged the war in Ukraine and tensions in the Middle East to establish a yuan-denominated oil-trading bloc with Russia, Iran, and Saudi Arabia. In this way, Xi Jinping believes he has further distanced China from the U.S. dollar and any collateral threats of sanctions, making war over Taiwan ever more likely.

Joe Biden's strategic energy subservience has indeed put us once again at the mercy of a handful of large oil-producing nations that have one thing in common. Each views America as its enemy, and it is more than happy to use oil as a weapon to bring about our economic and national security demise and ring in a new multi-polar world.

The only way out now will be a quick return to strategic energy dominance. Here, "Green New Deal" Democrats must acknowledge that forcing the American people to reduce their demand for fossil fuels is a form of economic and national security suicide.

The greenhouse gas emissions math is simple. Whatever CO_2 reductions the American people might achieve through their sacrifices and massive subsidies will be offset more than tenfold by the emissions from the power plants and automobiles and factories of Communist China, India, and a whole host of developing nations—and their leaders will laugh at us all the way to the climate change bank.

The only way out is to put Donald Trump back in the White House. He will lead the charge to "drill baby, drill," while rebuilding the stability of our electricity grid through a range of policies identified in the next several chapters. In this way, strategic energy dominance in Trump's America will thereby enhance both our economic security and national security.

=========

CHAPTER 10

The Critical Importance of American Strategic Electricity Dominance

by Dave Walsh, retired president and CEO, Mitsubishi Power Systems Americas

The Biden regime has relentlessly pursued an "environmental only" approach to energy, joining only twelve nations in the world resolvedly on this same path. In hurtling down this climate crisis path, the U.S. government articulates no clarity toward the generation and distribution of abundant and cost-effective electricity.

The Bidenomics result has been the promotion of heavily subsidized investment in variable, nature-dependent electricity generation sources that are part-time and intermittent in nature. These sources are dangerously reliant on supply chains beyond U.S. borders that have high up-front capital costs.

For example, solar up-front capital costs are 4.5 times the equivalent cost of conventional combined cycle power generation.

specters of blackouts and brownouts inevitably rear their ugly heads on the hottest and coldest days, when power demand peaks.

More broadly, federal regulators are now warning of similar types of electricity shortages emerging soon across much of our regional transmission system.

For example, under the Green New Deal banner and related heavy Environmental Protection Agency (EPA) and Securities and Exchange Commission (SEC) regulatory influence, the Midcontinent Independent System Operator (MISO) and PJM Interconnection (PJM) serving some twenty-three states have seen generation utilities, reacting to both the EPA and Environmental, Social, and Governance (ESG) shareholders, prematurely shuttered very significant capacity from coal and nuclear plants. This full-time, dispatchable electricity has been displaced by very part-time wind and solar power resources, dramatically increasing the fragility of our transmission systems.

Bidenomics is similarly strangling oil and gas generation. The Biden regime has shut down federal land oil leases in the Gulf of Mexico, Alaska, and elsewhere—curiously in lock step with announced production cutbacks by Saudi Arabia and OPEC. The Biden regime has also imposed pipeline restrictions while its Environmental Protection Agency has developed onerous nitrogen oxide standards that will severely curtail natural gas–fired generation while raising its cost.

Communist China has predictably reacted to this situation by continuing to harangue the United States, Europe, and much of the rest of the world to achieve net-zero carbon policies through the procurement of Chinese-produced EVs, lithium-ion batteries, and thin film PV solar panels. In effect, Biden's Green New Deal is the full employment act for Chinese sweatshops. Meanwhile, both hypocrisy and irony are in no small shortage.

Communist China hypocritically continues to build an astonishing two new coal plants *per week*, building out their own necessary baseload continuous duty electricity system, while generating more carbon dioxide than all OECD nations combined!

On the irony front, the greener Joe Biden seeks to make America, the more dependent this nation becomes on a coterie of rogue nations out to destroy America—from the aforementioned Communist China to the oil-producing nations of Russia, Iran, and Venezuela.

The Pollyannish policy initiatives of the Biden regime now targeting the abandonment of fossil fuels, which are currently fully 92 percent of all U.S. energy use, are based on the false hope that somehow America's industrial base and economy can survive this transition. It is beyond foolhardy.

A second Trump administration will immediately refocus on a diverse energy and electricity strategy that leverages the abundance of America's fossil fuels. Through appropriate executive orders, presidential memoranda, and sound personnel choices within key bureaucracies, the Trump administration should

- Recommit to proven energy production of all types while prioritizing the highest energy density, twenty-four hours a day domestic electricity generators.
- Institute a moratorium for the foreseeable future in the permanent shutdown of any more baseload plants of any kind.

- Abandon once again the sovereign nation–limiting Paris Climate Accords (PCA), whose environmental targets we've largely achieved. The PCA incredibly includes an obligation to pay the country with the world's second-largest military and economy (China) billions to clean its coal plants.
- Remove unaffordable tax incentives and development programs supporting now-mature energy resources, economically and technically challenged carbon capture systems, and the related transmission of all manners of power.
- Support the reemergence of baseload, full-time dispatchable power generation technology and the construction of badly needed additional U.S. refining capacity. '
- Remove buying and manufacturing incentives favoring one type of vehicle and any household product over others, based on fuel or battery type or efficiency, and once again allow consumer preferences to prevail.
- Modify EPA standards targeting the elimination of the use of, or making intentionally cost-prohibitive, certain baseload electricity sources and natural gas and oil-based products.
- Free up domestic gas and oil production on federal lands and in the Gulf of Mexico.
- Approve the Keystone Excel pipeline and other pipeline transmissions required to allow the free and demonstrably safer flow of pipeline gas and oil to American end users.
- Reinvigorate U.S.-based uranium supply and processing, now some 52 percent emanating from Russia and allied states.
- Direct the Nuclear Regulatory Commission to work to reduce the cost of new advanced and small modular reactors. '
- Direct the Department of Energy to revisit clean, ultra-

supercritical (HECA) Western coal technology as has been widely applied in Japan, China, and Germany.
- Remove all Securities and Exchange Commission and other agency regulations now supporting Environmental, Social, and Governance (ESG) investing, i.e., anti-energy investing.

CHAPTER 11

Your Volvo May Be
a Chinese Spy

People who drive electric vehicles love the high-tech feel of their cockpits. Tesla cars famously feature huge monitors with a myriad of data displays and controls that make you feel like you might be in a flight simulator. These screens allow users to do everything from managing the cabin climate to playing video games—connecting Xbox or PS4 game controllers to the car is actually an option. The powerful processors in these cars are on par with those high-end game consoles. These systems connect to every part of the car and provide a seamless computing platform that allows the driver to monitor and control the vehicle from battery performance to security. Newer models even use a touch screen control for shifting (forward, reverse, park).

These sophisticated computing systems are connected to

a myriad of sensors, including GPS location, and multiple live cameras inside and outside the cabin, along with microphones for voice recognition controls. The Tesla website brags, "This system provides a view of the world that a driver alone cannot access, seeing in every direction simultaneously, and on wavelengths that go far beyond the human senses." These sensors are designed to support advanced safety systems like automatic emergency braking and collision avoidance. They also allow some vehicles to actually drive themselves—currently under driver supervision.

It is also important to note that Teslas and many other vehicles are persistently connected to the company, the owner, and the Internet via cellular and Wi-Fi networks. These connections allow for streaming media (you can watch Netflix in your Tesla), continual updates for the navigation systems, software patches, and security monitoring. A Tesla owner can access video from their car live from anywhere on Earth and get security alerts if the cameras see unusual events. Tesla also collects data for improving the driving experience, and most importantly for perfecting the self-driving technologies. This connection is two-way, and the owner can control the car as well, including unlocking it or even starting it for someone else to drive as needed. Tesla's "summon" mode allows the user to call the car to them with their phone, and it will drive itself out of their garage or across a parking lot to pick them up.

While this is very cool tech, China began to restrict the use of Tesla's EVs by governmental officials a few years ago and the CCP has increasingly restricted the American firm's cars from entering governmental compounds and military complexes. Why? Because, in many ways, a modern EV is more of a computing platform with motors and wheels attached than a car with a computer added on. China has asserted that American EVs could be collecting data on facilities and individuals and providing that to America's spies, and it has even temporarily banned them from resorts when China's leaders gather. Tesla being the only U.S. automaker with significant EV market penetration in China, it has been the major concern for China's paranoid rulers.

The Boys from Beijing may be paranoid, but they are also smart and unscrupulous. While there is no evidence that American cars are spying on anyone, if China's intelligence agencies understand that an EV can be turned into a mobile spybot, then you can bet your bottom dollar they are doing it themselves. China began requiring all car manufacturers, European and American included, to share data with their government years ago. A 2018 story from the Australian Broadcasting Corporation reported that "Over 200 car manufacturers are sending real-time location information and dozens of other data points from electric vehicles in China to surveillance centers backed by the country's government." High-tech cars in China are now an important part of the CCP's domestic spying and social control agenda and they are happily exporting that to the United States.

Chinese electric cars have recently begun to enter the U.S. market under the Volvo moniker*. Despite its Swedish history, Volvo Cars was sold by Ford to China's Geely Automotive in 2010. Geely manufactures Volvo EVs in China. Together they control the high-end EV brand Polestar, also made in China. BYD and

---

* Volvo Cars is distinct from the larger AB Volvo industrial firm, which makes trucks and more.

other Chinese brands are likely to enter the American market very soon. There is a general expectation/fear in the automotive business that Chinese EVs are about to pour into the United States and sweep aside the more expensive and less successful battery-powered efforts of incumbent American firms like GM and Ford.

Even the EV-happy Biden White House has been unable to hide from this clear threat, and in February 2024 they ordered the Department of Commerce to investigate the threat and "consider regulations to address those threats." A statement from Biden clearly states, "China's policies could flood our market with its vehicles, posing risks to our national security."

The second Trump administration will go further than this and issue a ban on the importation of electronic devices, including smart cars (EV or not), that transmit data to servers in China or allow for control or software updates from China. This should include products like UAV drones.

Again, China understands the breadth of the broader electronic device threat and has recently implemented restrictions prohibiting Apple's made-in-China iPhones from entering governmental buildings because of their connectivity to the United States. That's richly ironic given Apple's unwillingness to work with U.S. authorities and craven pandering to the demands of the Chinese police state. However, knowing this and understanding China's control over their domestic firms, it is a safe bet that every Huawei and Xiaomi mobile phone in America is a current or potential spy for China. Until President Trump resumes his office and takes action, it would be best to trash those devices.

CHAPTER 12

Toward a Rational Federal Lands Policy and Return to Strategic Energy Dominance

by David Bernhardt, former secretary of the Interior

President Trump views energy production as vital for America's economy and national security. During his first term, he focused on expanding sensible energy development from all sources.

Thanks to President Trump's leadership, the U.S. Department of the Interior (DOI) made sweeping regulatory changes to foster a thriving economy and safer communities. The DOI unleashed responsible onshore and offshore energy development, prioritized worker safety, expanded outdoor recreation access and conservation, strengthened cultural resource protections, and supported tribal economic development.

These reforms expanded the energy renaissance from private to federal lands—increasing American energy production considerably. Through such reforms, the federal government made getting drilling permits faster and easier, opened more land to energy production, and maintained environmental safeguards.

Under President Trump, America began producing more energy than it consumed—making America energy independent for the first time since the 1950s—while establishing America's strategic energy dominance. Not coincidentally, gasoline prices remained low throughout his term.

The Trump reforms impacting the DOI's managed lands were indeed important actions. More than 20 percent of the nation's oil and 12 percent of U.S. natural gas come from these lands and waters, along with more than 40 percent of coal production.

Regrettably, as soon as Joe Biden became president, he reversed course, prioritizing climate activism over energy independence. Influenced by the radical Left and the Green New Deal, this radical Biden regime has left no stone unturned to restrict American oil and gas production.

On the very first day of the Biden regime, the DOI's acting leadership revoked the authority of all subordinates to "issue any onshore or offshore fossil fuel authorization" for new operations. Biden's secretary of the Interior also moved quickly to curtail energy production.

In addition, less than two weeks after taking office, Biden's DOI revoked directives that expedited DOI permitting, promoted oil and gas development on federal lands, streamlined environmental reviews, expanded offshore energy production, and promoted U.S. energy independence. At Biden's direction, the DOI also suspended oil and gas leasing in the small portions of the Arctic National Wildlife Refuge that had been open to drilling.

Biden's Green New Deal policies provide a very raw deal for every American consumer, business, and energy worker. In a second term, Donald Trump will promptly reverse course by rescinding these Biden orders while reestablishing the Trump administration orders that were focused on improving transparency, expanding energy actions, and reducing unneeded red tape.

Completing such actions will hardly be the end of the effort. President Trump's secretary of Interior should lead the effort to revise regulations related to oil and gas on federal lands, repeal unreasonable limits on the use of public lands, improve the implementation of the Endangered Species Act, and expand access to our nation's mineral resources.

In the spirit of the admonition that "personnel is policy," Trump's DOI secretary should also ensure that the DOI includes within its political ranks only those who fully support the policy vision of the president and who understand the need to promptly drive fundamental change to secure better outcomes for the American people.

Finally, during the Trump administration, DOI successfully established the Bureau of Land Management's (BLM) headquarters in Colorado, bringing its leadership closer to its assets in western states. This realignment repositioned it to better respond to the needs of the American people. While the Biden Administration has repeatedly worked to frustrate this effort, a second Trump administration will quickly consider reversing course, thereby ensuring the bureaucracy is closer to the American people it serves.

CHAPTER 13

The Crisis at Our Southern Border

by Mark Morgan, former acting commissioner of Customs and Border Protection and chief of the U.S. Border Patrol in Trump Administration

We are in the midst of an undeniable self-inflicted border security crisis, which is jeopardizing our country's sovereignty, safety, and national security. The Biden administration and radical politicians in Washington, D.C., have methodically and intentionally created a man-made disaster on our southern border unparalleled in our nation's history. Guided by the most ideological and partisan aims, these feckless politicians have opened our borders to an invasion of illegal aliens. They have done this by purposefully dismantling every meaningful border security measure previously in place. The results were predictable: in thirty-six months, Customs and Border Protection encountered 9.1 million illegal and inadmissible aliens at our borders. The unconscionable reality is that President

Biden, along with his accomplice, Secretary Mayorkas, have willfully rendered our borders meaningless and left our nation more vulnerable than we were prior to 9/11.

The premise of how we look at and discuss the unmitigated chaos and lawlessness at our borders is generally misleading, uninformed, and forces a faulty binary choice upon the American people. It's being presented this way by design. In today's politically and ideologically charged environment, they have intentionally blurred the lines between *legal* and *illegal* immigration. Additionally, most of our collective bandwidth is spent characterizing the plight of immigrants as simply "looking for a better life," mandating we accept the "end justifies the means" argument for their violation of the law and the premise that *illegal* immigration is a victimless crime. If we don't accept this factually devoid narrative, we're eviscerated as anti-immigrant and labeled as racists. It's just simply not true.

The reality is when policies open our borders in a blatant effort to incentivize, encourage, and facilitate illegal immigration, our borders also become increasingly open and vulnerable to the vast and complex set of ever-changing threats facing our nation from outside its borders. These threats are not mutually exclusive—they are in fact interconnected. Thus, when we discuss illegal immigration, it's essential we do so with the understanding of how it degrades our ability to effectively protect, defend, and secure our border, as well as the corresponding erosion of the rule of law and impact on our nation's sovereignty. If our borders are less secure, ergo our national security.

For decades the Mexican cartels have taken advantage of every gap and loophole made available through weak, ambiguous, and faulty U.S. policy. They are masters at exploitation. These organizations are sophisticated with a proven capacity to evolve in response to our county's change in policies—constantly adapting their techniques, tactics, and procedures in an effort to maximize their profit, leverage, power, influence, and strength. And that's exactly what they've done. Following the 2020 election, with the Biden administration's clear intentions to open the floodgates to illegal aliens, the cartels heard the call loud and clear. They immediately began to shift resources in an effort to build up their human smuggling operations. Unlike narcotic smuggling, exploiting human beings for the cartels is a low-risk, high-reward endeavor. It didn't take long for the billions in profits to come pouring in.

As U.S. law enforcement agencies are being forced to navigate the crushing volume of illegal aliens crossing our border, in many areas the majority of Border Patrol agents are pulled off the front lines, away from their law enforcement and national security mission, as they're relegated to administrative processing duties; serving as a federal travel agency with the cartels as their sole client. With a dramatically reduced enforcement capability, our government has enabled the cartels to easily expand their operational control of large areas of the unmanned border, along with their capacity to smuggle in deadly drugs, criminals, and national security threats undetected.

You don't have to be a rocket scientist to understand the correlation—having millions of illegal aliens pushed to our borders overwhelms our frontline personnel and creates the perfect storm for the cartels to exploit. Not only are they profiting from the increased flow of their human smuggling operations, an annual multi-billion-dollar criminal enterprise, but they force the same illegal aliens to be used as "distraction pawns." With border patrol resources preoccupied fulfilling their new mission as a "processing enterprise" we've actually made it easier for the cartels to sneak other dangerous and deadly threats into our country, as well as exponentially increase the likelihood of "gotaways"—illegal aliens who sneak past our frontline resources and avoid apprehension.

There have been an estimated 1.9 million known "gotaways" in the first three years of the Biden administration—equivalent to the population of Idaho. And anyone who dares suggest that there are bad people among those illegally entering our country are ruthlessly demonized to cover up the harsh truth and silence them. The reality is that there are criminals breaking into our country. Many have been convicted or charged with violent offenses and are considered dangerous predators. Included in the almost two million illegal aliens who have avoided apprehension are rapists, murderers, pedophiles, drug and weapon smugglers, gang members, and national security threats.

Just within the past three years, CBP has encountered more than 130,000 criminal aliens and violent gang members. In 2023, Immigration and Customs Enforcement arrested more than 73,000 criminal illegal aliens inside the United States, including 1,713 murderers and 33,209 other violent offenders. During the same time period, Border Patrol has apprehended illegal aliens from 180 different countries, many of which we know sponsor, harbor, and facilitate terrorism, as well as nations that pose a significant risk to our economic security. Under the Biden administration we've encountered more Chinese nationals and illegal aliens on the FBI's Watch List than in any other time in our nation's history. The Watch-Listed aliens represent a 3,000 percent increase compared to the same time frame under the Trump administration. When we assess the "gotaways" in the backdrop of who we know is crossing our borders, the question isn't if or when the threat enters our country, the issue is, it's already here.

By now, everyone is aware of the fentanyl crisis gripping our nation, the leading cause of death among those eighteen to forty-five years of age. In 2023, the overdose/poisoning rate topped 112,000 for the first time, according to the Center for Disease Control; more than the deaths America has suffered from every terrorist attack on our homeland, as well as the Vietnam, Iraq, and Afghanistan wars combined. However, what receives little air time, in a continuing effort to downplay the magnitude concerning the collapse of our border, is the fact that the overwhelming majority of drugs in this country emanate from Mexico and cross through our wide-open southwest border at an increasingly alarming rate. It's a guarantee, if you have a methamphetamine overdose or fentanyl-related death in your neighborhood, it's connected to our border, of which we've handed over operational control to the cartels.

Border security and illegal immigration have become one of the most politically driven, emotionally charged, and ideology-based issues in recent history. As I watch politicians, the mainstream media, as well as the current administration provide their version of what's happening at our southern border, it's impossible for the American people to separate fact from fiction. I've been serving this country for more than thirty-five years, under six different administrations—both Republican and Democrat. While unfortunately I've become numb over the years to the spin and misdirection that has become part of the day-to-day operations in Washington, I have never seen an intentional campaign so blatantly mislead and out-right lie to the American people as I've seen under the Biden administration. It's not enough that they are attempting to redefine morality and American values to fit neatly into their current narrative as part of their strategy to ensure permanent political power. They are creating their own reality, reshaping history, intentionally driving false narratives, and forcing the American people to surrender to their distorted perspective—you either want to help poor immigrants looking for a better life or you're an uncompassionate, uncaring racist. If we don't fall in line with the radical, false, dangerous narrative, they attempt to silence us.

Mayorkas continues to defiantly and arrogantly opine our "borders are secure" and our "borders are closed." It's an un-equivocal lie and he knows it. He has violated the law, refuses to enforce the law, and consistently abuses his authorities. It's a feeble attempt to deflect responsibility, downplay the severity of the crisis, and convince the American people to keep "fiddling while Rome burns."

In 2014, then Vice-President Biden was a fierce advocate of increased enforcement, detention, and removal strategies to address the declared humanitarian crisis that pales in compari-son to what has been unleased against our country these past three years. What happened to that Biden? His blatant reversal and repudiation of his own words, ideology, and actions rep-resents the quintessential political charlatan that unabashedly and with ease can change their deepest held beliefs, as easily as a chameleon changes their color, if it will bestow the power unto them they so desperately crave. President Biden's once firmly held beliefs concerning the importance of detention and enhanced removal, as well as America's innate responsibility to prevent migrants from being exploited on their journey to the United States, were replaced with whatever he needed to say to get elected.

Laken Riley. Say her name.

CHAPTER 14

Securing Our Borders: Every Town in America Is Now a Border Town

Under the policies of Joe Biden, America, with a population of roughly 330 million, now has the most open border of any major nation in the world. Meanwhile, much of the rest of the world—with a population of nearly eight *billion*—would love to come to America. What could go wrong here? Plenty!

During the Biden regime, more than 2 million illegal aliens have flooded across America's southern border. Most are poorly educated males now pushing down the wages of Black, brown, and blue-collar Americans. Far too many are children now toiling in the factories of American corporations—the number of unaccompanied minors crossing into Joe Biden's America last year hit a record 130,000.

With drug cartel couriers, gang members, terrorists, and child traffickers notable exceptions, these illegal immigrants are not demons. They are rational humans simply seeking a better life. Yet, absent a secure border policy, unrestrained immigration will make the vast majority of Americans worse off.

To understand the toxic politics of Biden's open borders policies, one need only understand the late professor James Q. Wilson's principle of "concentrated benefits, diffuse costs." To wit: Where policy benefits accrue to powerful special interests and costs are spread across America's population, the special interests typically win.

Millions of Main Street Americans now bear the diffuse costs of illegal immigration through higher crime, rising drug use, and fentanyl carnage. Our schools are increasingly overcrowded, emergency rooms double as pediatric wards, and middle-class taxpayers shoulder the lion's share of the burdens associated with subsidizing a significant fraction of the illegal immigrant population.

In addition, these poorly educated, low-skilled illegals do indeed depress wages in the lower ends of the labor market—the Federal Reserve has even perversely noted the phenomenon as an aid to fighting inflation. American workers most at risk from poverty are also most likely to lose their jobs to this "illegal immigrant army of the newly employed."

Most controversial, there are second- and third-order effects on American culture, politics, religion, and society that may become toxic. Here, while Judeo-Christian America used to be a melting pot, it is becoming increasingly Balkanized.

As foreign-origin religious, nationalist, and ethnic groups take over large swaths of American cities and suburbs, they stick far more to themselves than integrate into the American way of life while using our ballot boxes to "vote for their own." How this "America last" turn of the immigration screw ends is very much an open question, yet it is a question that should be asked—and answered—in any rational border discussion.

Even as these costs are diffused across America, the benefits from this border invasion are highly concentrated. Here, labor is certainly cheaper, and American corporations—from General Motors, General Mills, and Frito-Lay to Ford, J.Crew, Walmart, and even the "woke" Ben & Jerry's—are jumping at the opportunity to employ docile children who will make few demands in the workplace.

It's not just corporate executives and their Wall Street financiers who love open borders. Democrats are making a big bet that these new arrivals will vote Democrat if they gain citizenship—now you also understand the demands for amnesty.

To this political end, the Bidenites are systematically shipping many new arrivals to red states. They hope these political time bombs will blow up Republican control of America's MAGA heartland.

Serving the Trump administration, I played a small role in helping secure our border. While it took some time to overcome a labyrinth of Democrat judge-rendered legal opinions favoring open borders and child trafficking, President Trump finally did so.

Under the threat of massive tariffs, Mexico and the Northern Triangle countries of El Salvador, Guatemala, and Honduras all signed "safe third nation" agreements. With such agreements—Joe Biden immediately ended each—these countries agreed to hold illegals on *their* side of the border until any claims for entering the United States were processed.

Such processing takes months if not years so these safe third nation agreements not only prevented illegals from entering the United States, but they discouraged migrants from crashing our borders at all.

It should be clear America's current border invasion is a politician-made disaster. It is manufactured largely by K Street lobbyists of the D.C. swamp, corporate donors who buy up our congressmen, and a Democratic party that has embraced an open border strategy to reign politically supreme.

Elections do indeed have consequences. Now, we must throw the open-border rascals out. Here's the "Action, Action, Action" plan:

- To protect American economic and national security, it is the policy of the United States to secure its borders and promptly deport all illegal aliens.
- President Trump built more than 450 miles of border wall in his first term. He will complete that wall in his second term.

President Trump should also

- Restore safe third-nation agreements with Mexico and the Northern Triangle countries of El Salvador, Guatemala, and Honduras and pursue additional agreements with the remaining countries of Central and South America.
- Once again end "catch and release" practices, eliminate asylum fraud, and crack down on "birth tourism."
- Immediately begin the mass deportation of all illegal aliens

that have entered the United States and engage the U.S. military to secure our southern border.

- Ensure that all U.S. Customs and Border Protection agents will be treated with the dignity and respect they deserve.

In cooperative states, President Trump can even deputize the National Guard and local law enforcement to assist with rapidly removing illegal alien gang members and criminals.

President Trump will also take down the drug cartels and human traffickers just as he took down ISIS. An action plan may look like this:

- Impose a total naval embargo on cartels.
- Order the Department of Defense to inflict maximum damage on cartel leadership.
- Designate cartels as Foreign Terrorist Organizations and choke off their access to the global financial system.
- Get the full cooperation of neighboring governments to dismantle the cartels, or else expose every bribe and kickback that allows these criminal networks to preserve their brutal reign.
- Ask Congress to ensure that drug smugglers and traffickers can receive the death penalty. When President Trump is back in the White House, the drug kingpins and vicious traffickers will never sleep soundly again.

President Trump will also deliver a merit-based immigration system that protects American labor, promotes American values, and contributes to, rather than subtracts from, national prosperity.

CHAPTER 15

Stopping the Deadly Flood of Communist Chinese Fentanyl

In January 2021, the Biden regime opened the floodgates on our southern border. Not coincidentally, fentanyl deaths across the United States have spiked like never before—and are at their *highest* levels in our nation's history, killing tens of thousands of Americans annually. Indeed, fentanyl is currently the leading cause of death for adults between the ages of eighteen and forty-five.

Communist China is responsible for at least 90 percent of illicit fentanyl found in the United States. Because Biden blew the doors off borders, this deadly poison even more freely makes its way to America. With deadly consequences, this killer drug corrupts the bodies of innocent children and adults—it looks like fruity, rainbow, candy eye droppers and nasal sprays. As a lethal cocktail, it is sometimes even mixed with other harmful drugs.

During Joe Biden's first term, tens of thousands of pounds of fentanyl have been seized at the southern border. At *least* 1.4 million illegal immigrants who arrived at the southern border since 2021 have been classified as "gotaways," meaning they were not apprehended by U.S. Customs and Border Protection (CBP) and freely entered our country. With this many gotaways, who knows how many *more* tens of thousands of pounds actually *entered* our country, on their way to kill tens of thousands.

For Communist China, killing Americans is big business. It has a robust pharmaceutical manufacturing industry and is responsible for producing 80 percent of the active pharmaceutical ingredients (APIs)—a form of precursor material—in American medicines. When it comes to illicit fentanyl found in America, more than 99 percent of its precursor materials are produced in Communist China.

Once these precursor materials are produced, they are shipped to Mexico—usually directly into the hands of the Jalisco New Generation (CJNG) and Sinaloa Cartel groups. Next, the cartels manufacture the fentanyl precursors into fentanyl-containing pills inside illegal labs. From there, they smuggle the finished poison product all the way across our southern border.

Senator Pete Ricketts of Nebraska admitted that during his last two years as governor during the Biden regime in 2021 and 2022, he saw the amount of fentanyl, methamphetamines, and cocaine in Nebraska double, triple, and eventually *quadruple* as a result of the Biden administration's lax border policies. With a surge of migrants down south, CBP has become overwhelmed and distracted; it is easier now than ever to smuggle drugs into our country.

The greatest irony is that when it comes to domestically trafficked illicit drugs in their own country, the Chinese Communist Party (CCP) pulls no punches. In fact, Chinese—and foreign—drug traffickers are sentenced to years of imprisonment and even death when caught. Yet, the CCP freely allows their domestic drug criminals to engage with cartels in Mexico to spread deadly fentanyl to America.

Sadly for Americans and their families, the CCP does not respect Joe Biden enough to make any serious attempt to fix their fentanyl problem. Under President Trump in 2018, the CCP restricted the domestic production and sale of two of the most common ingredients for fentanyl, scheduled dozens of fentanyl derivatives for government regulation, and ordered Chinese law enforcement to arrest manufacturers of certain strands of fentanyl-containing substances outside of the CCP's fentanyl regulatory network.

Under President Biden in 2022, the CCP announced it stopped all talks and cooperation with the United States regarding counternarcotics and drug trafficking. A strong and well-respected leader is needed now more than ever before, in order to save Americans from this crisis.

President Trump's first-term actions of building the wall, closing down our border to criminals, and forcing Communist China to crack down on its own domestic fentanyl operations resulted in tens of thousands of pounds of opioids seized at the southern border, the dismantling of more than three thousand drug trafficking organizations, as well as seizing all of their fentanyl, which would have killed 105,000 Americans, the indictment of several major Chinese drug trafficking criminals, and much more.

In 2025, during his first week as president, Donald Trump will initiate sweeping measures to stop the fentanyl carnage. He will inflict maximum damage on drug cartel operations utilizing robust U.S. military assets and seek the death penalty for convicted drug dealers and human traffickers.

These actions will enable the United States to respond to fentanyl trafficking with the full force of the U.S. government and its federal agencies, including gathering intelligence and strike options for the U.S. military—for example, striking Mexican fentanyl labs.

President Trump should also

- Designate fentanyl as a weapon of mass destruction—which the attorneys general from nearly twenty different states have called for—and designate Mexican and Communist Chinese drug cartels as terrorist groups.
- Develop new techniques to detect sources of fentanyl production and trafficking.
- Improve care for American victims struggling with addiction through federally funded rehabilitation programs, mental health counseling, and other holistic care options.

CHAPTER 16

Declaring War on the Drug Cartels and Child Traffickers

Mexico is home to the five largest and most deadly drug cartels in the entire world: the Guadalajara, Sinaloa, Tijuana, Juarez, and Gulf cartels.

These merchants of death are directly responsible for the deaths of *tens of thousands* of Americans each year because of their dark and dirty drug trafficking operations. This is on top of the rapes, killing, and trafficking of their own women and children.

During the Biden regime, more than a quarter of a million Americans have died from drugs. More broadly, more Americans die each year from the poison these cartels traffic than the entire Vietnam War combined.

This is not strictly a Mexican enterprise. Each of these major cartels is in direct partnership with the Communist Party of China.

The CCP and its illicit drug manufacturers ship in vast quantities of the building block materials for deadly fentanyl.

Make no mistake about this: Chinese Communist chemicals are made into finished pills inside illicit cartel labs in Mexico. From these labs, a human army of cartel mules, many of them women and children, are used to smuggle this fentanyl over the southern border to kill Americans.

Under a new Trump presidency, any group that kills Americans will be designated an enemy of the United States, and any group partnered with the CCP will be considered an enemy of the United States. These enemies will be met with the full force of U.S. federal law enforcement and intelligence agencies and our military.

Regrettably, the Biden regime has adopted the opposite policy. Indeed, since the beginning of the Biden regime, the CCP and Mexican government have publicly proclaimed they will stop cooperating with U.S. intelligence and law enforcement to prevent illicit drug trafficking—particularly fentanyl—over the U.S. border.

For example, in 2022, the CCP published a statement that it would suspend all of its counternarcotic and law enforcement cooperation with the United States. In 2021, the Mexican government declared the Mérida Initiative—the $3 billion U.S.-Mexico security cooperation framework to stop drug trafficking in place since the Bush administration—completely "dead."

Likewise, in 2022, President Andrés Manuel López Obrador went even further: He falsely denied that fentanyl is produced in Mexico, despite admissions of this fact by his own government.

These bold pronouncements *alone* highlight the disgraceful weakness of Joe Biden and his open-border policies. President Xi and President López Obrador wouldn't have dared to behave this brazenly when President Trump was in office, which is why it never happened under his first term.

Under the Trump administration in 2020, the Department of Homeland Security deported more than four thousand illegal alien gang members and stopped hundreds more from entering the country. In sharp contrast, in Joe Biden's America, Mexican cartels have established criminal networks within the United States with American street, prison, and motorcycle gangs. These cartels even send their own Mexican gang members into the United States to carry out violent missions.

Note here that Mexican drug cartels are notorious for inflicting physical violence not just on unarmed Mexicans but on American citizens as well. Some recent examples include the 2019 killing of *nine* Americans in Sonora, Mexico, by the Juarez Cartel, where three women and six children were gunned down in an attempted ambush of rival Sinaloa operatives; the 2023 Gulf Cartel murder of two Americans; and a horrific gunshot injury on one American.

Despite Biden's hapless Attorney General Merrick Garland's strong words proclaiming the Biden administration will be "ruthless" in pursuing the Mexican cartel culprits responsible for the most recent American deaths, all that culminated was a laughable travel advisory by the Biden State Department, warning Americans to not travel to Mexico. This was quickly ridiculed by Mexican President López Obrador, who threw back in Joe Biden's face high crime rates in the United States.

It's not just drugs killing Americans that are the problem. Mexico's cartels engage in some of the worst human rights violations in the world. On average, 60 percent of children caught by cartels are used for drug smuggling and forced into child pornography. Girls as young as *five years old* are being raped.

Drug cartels have even created "rape trees," where they rape women and children approaching the southern border and kill them. These sociopaths then hang the rape victims' garments on nearby trees to taunt our border agents.

The problems posed by Mexico's cartels are deep and systemic. Yet, as bad as they are, they have been made infinitely worse by a weak Biden open-border policy. Biden's open borders, coupled with weakened law enforcement and a hopelessly woke military leadership, have encouraged—indeed, encouraged!—more than three million illegal aliens to enter our country. This border invasion has provided Mexico's criminal enterprises with cover and thereby allowed them to operate freely on U.S. soil.

In his second term, President Trump will indeed wage war on the Mexican drug cartels just like he did during his first term. To do this, President Trump should

- Direct the U.S. Department of State to designate Chinese and Mexican drug cartel groups as foreign terrorist organizations.
- Label fentanyl and other illicit drugs trafficked over the border as weapons of mass destruction.
- Provide a whole-of-government strategic and tactical response to the crisis utilizing our law enforcement, intelligence, and military.
- Empower the U.S. military to use the Army Special Forces and the intelligence community to conduct targeted strikes and intelligence operations against Mexican drug cartels

and their leaders to eviscerate them as quickly and efficiently as possible.

- Direct U.S. law enforcement agencies, such as the Department of Justice, to capture and harshly prosecute Mexican cartel groups operating in the United States, in addition to prosecuting Americans who willingly partner with them.

CHAPTER 17

Disarming a Weaponized Department of (In)Justice and FBI

by Mike Davis, founder and president, Article III Project (A3P)

President Trump's mission to drain the swamp in D.C. has been met with relentless fury from the swamp monsters. Nowhere has this fury been more in evidence than at a partisan and weaponized Department of (In)Justice and FBI, which have been on a nonstop witch hunt to find a crime, any crime, with which to charge Donald Trump since he embarked on his political journey in 2015.

Through investigations conducted by Congressional Republicans and by John Durham, we've discovered just how frequently the Department of Justice has flagrantly broken rules and norms to unfairly and unjustly target Trump.

It started in 2016 when the FBI was desperate to spy on Trump's campaign as it gained momentum. It was the Durham report that revealed that going after Trump's 2016 campaign foreign policy adviser Carter Page was a "top priority" for FBI Director James Comey—the fish does rot from the top, as the proverb says.

As Durham's report noted, top brass within the FBI, starting with Comey, "constantly pressured" leadership to get a Foreign Intelligence Surveillance Act (FISA) warrant to spy on Page—a bogus warrant that would include seventeen significant omissions.

These Trump witch hunts would continue into the Trump administration in 2017 with the effort to set up the president's national security adviser General Michael Flynn and entrap him in a non-crime. At the same time, a stream of leaks sought to undermine the White House's ability to enact policy by trying to falsely portray Trump as a puppet of Russian president Vladimir Putin.

Just take a look at how the *Washington Post* covered Trump's 2017 decision to stop the CIA from arming Islamists in Syria. The *Post* first wrote:

> *President Trump has decided to end the CIA's covert program to arm and train moderate Syrian rebels battling the government of Bashar al-Assad, a move long sought by Russia, according to U.S. officials.*

A year later when Trump withdrew troops from Syria, the *Washington Post*'s headline was: "Trump's decision to withdraw from Syria marks a win for Putin."

Ironically, instead of President Trump scoring bipartisan foreign policy wins with traditionally anti-war Democrats for his troop withdrawals and quest to end America's endless wars, those Democrats became rabidly pro-war. As Glenn Greenwald documented in a 2019 column, Democrats during the Trump presidency became "far more militaristic and pro-war than Republicans."

The DOJ's fight against President Trump hasn't been about stopping a man so much as it has been about stopping the movement he leads. That effort continues to this day as President Trump remains under a swarm of DOJ investigations and indictments.

The not-so-hidden DOJ agenda is to derail Trump's 2024 run for the presidency. This Jack Smith jackal-led effort seeks to either jail Trump or heap so much mud on him that he will surrender his frontrunner status and fall out of contention. Of course—and much to the consternation of his persecutors—Trump only rises in the polls with each new phony indictment.

DOJ's dirty hands and fingerprints are also all over Manhattan district attorney Alvin Bragg and his indictment of President Trump. In December 2020, the George Soros–funded Bragg hired top Biden DOJ political appointee and longtime Democrat activist Matthew Colangelo to help run his unprecedented political prosecution of Biden's top political enemy.

Colangelo is a lifelong leftwing activist with stints working as an adviser to Barack Obama and as an aide to former DNC chair Tom Perez. Colangelo never served as a line prosecutor or defense attorney. He is simply a senior Democrat operative the DOJ placed in Bragg's office to get Trump.

Clearly, disarming a politically weaponized DOJ will be a top priority for the second Trump administration. President Trump will clean house of Democratic operatives masking as career federal government employees. He will also aggressively pursue Democrat politicians and their liberal allies, whose crimes the Biden Justice Department has ignored—starting with Hunter Biden and Russian hoax perpetrators with names like Comey, Clapper, Brennan, Page, and Strzok.

We can only right their wrongs by giving them a taste of their own medicine. This is the "dead chicken strategy," as once explained to me by Supreme Court justice Clarence Thomas.

When he was growing up, Thomas learned that to stop dogs from killing chickens, they would take those chickens and wrap them around the dogs' necks. And as those chickens rotted around those dogs' necks, those dogs lost the taste for chicken. That's what President Trump must do to the left in his second term.

On day one, President Trump should immediately

- Audit all open FBI investigations and terminate any that are unlawful and against the national interest and publish a report outlining these decisions.
- Identify and fire DOJ/FBI employees who have participated in anti-Catholic, anti–pro-life, and anti-Trump investigations.
- Open investigations into Antifa and other groups responsible for unlawful protests outside Supreme Court justices' homes and prosecute the Antifa terrorists who burned down American cities.
- Submit a legislative proposal to Congress to eliminate the ten-year term for the FBI director and limit it to five years.
- Renew the federal criminal law enforcement commitment to preserving law and order in lawless inner cities where local, often Soros-funded, prosecutors refuse to protect American citizens through law enforcement.

They are an astonishing eleven times higher for battery storage and offshore wind power.

A sound electricity strategy under a new Trump administration will feature the diversification of American resources and abundant, cost-effective energy supporting economic vitality, affordability, and national defense. This is precisely the kind of strategy Donald Trump relied on during his first term to make this American nation a net exporter of energy for the first time in twenty-five years.

During President Trump's first term, natural gas, oil, and petroleum-related products reached some $350 billion of our $2 trillion in annual exports. A key factor in this astonishing ascendance to strategic energy dominance—as well as providing a more reliable electricity grid—was this nation's fracking boom.

Historically, the United States has powered the electricity grid primarily by fossil fuels and nuclear power. Both coal and nuclear plants are key baseload providers, while clean, natural gas–fired generation has played critical roles in electricity generation from base, intermediate, and peak load plants.

As Green New Deal political forces have gained political power, there has been a concerted and successful effort to shutter both coal and nuclear plants. At the same time, the Biden regime's war on fracking has increasingly crippled coal and gas-fired generation.

Consider here that coal and nuclear plants yield electricity twenty-four hours a day, but land-based wind yields about eight hours and solar only about five hours nationally. This increased reliance on solar and wind has exposed Texas, California, MISO, and PJM to a substantial lack of electricity reserve margins. The

The 2024 Presidential Election as a Referendum on Whether to Imprison Donald Trump

What can Donald Trump and the American electorate learn from my (Peter Navarro) conviction for a crime I never should have been prosecuted for? Plenty, and these lessons have dire implications for the 2024 presidential election.

Lesson One: Elections can have consequences.

If Republicans controlled *either* the House of Representatives *or* the White House and Department of Justice (DOJ) after 2020, neither Donald Trump nor I would ever have been indicted. Instead, we have an uber-partisan, dual system of injustice under Joe Biden's banana republic rule interfering with, and thereby destroying faith in, our election and judicial systems.

Lesson Two: Judges have far more power to determine verdicts than juries.

In principle, every defendant is entitled to the broadest range of defenses. In practice, before a case gets to a jury, a judge can eliminate any number of defenses—or, in my case, almost *all.*

I was on trial for failing to comply with a Congressional subpoena. I have already made history as the first senior White House adviser in history *ever* to be so charged.

Memo to Merrick Garland: Your DOJ has a more than fifty-year policy that White House advisers and "alter egos" of the president like me *absolutely cannot be compelled to testify before Congress.* Despite my absolute testimonial immunity, Garland's weaponized DOJ went for my jugular.

The defenses I was stripped of by the judge ranged from unlawful bill of attainder and selective prosecution to entrapment by estoppel, public authority, and, most importantly, executive privilege. I was also denied numerous discovery requests that would have bolstered several defenses.

Donald Trump is unlikely to fare much better—and likely far worse.

Lesson Three: Any District of Columbia jury will be biased against Trump.

In my case, I sat through *voir dire* of fifty potential jurors drawn from D.C. voting rolls where Democrat registration runs at 76 percent, and Joe Biden got 92 percent of the 2020 vote. No potential juror expressed support for Trump. Many expressed anti-Trump sentiments. Yet, all jurors needed to do to be seated was swear their negative Trump views would not affect their verdict.

While I respect the twelve jurors who took time out of their busy days to do their civic duty, overcoming one's political biases is a lot to ask of human nature. This is particularly true when DOJ prosecutors play dirty pool—as they did in my case.

Lesson Four: DOJ prosecutors came to court not in search of justice but to put me in prison. Trump's prosecutors will likewise cheat and lie to make sure Trump is never again president.

In my case, rather than prove me guilty of the "crime" I was actually accused of—they couldn't even meet that burden—prosecutors John Crabbe and Elizabeth Aloi repeatedly sought to implant the false and prejudicial notion in the jury's mind that I was a "Trumpist insurrectionist" responsible for "fomenting" and "inciting" the January 6 violence.

In a darkly funny court moment, my attorney strenuously objected that Crabbe had cribbed the identical opening statement used in the Proud Boys and Oath Keepers cases. Despite such objections—and admonishments from the judge—Crabbe and Aloi would triple down on the January 6 and Trumpist red herrings as they themselves sought to foment and incite anger against me among jurors.

Tarred as I was with the Trump and January 6 brushes, I never had a chance. This was particularly true after a marshal inexplicably took my jurors outside the court building for some "fresh air." There, jurors bore witness to the foul sight of sign-wielding January 6 and anti-Trump protesters calling for my imprisonment. Within minutes of their return to deliberations, the jury would find me guilty. How do you spell *mistrial*?

Lesson Five: Add these four lessons up, and Donald Trump has zero chance of acquittal.

Accordingly, the 2024 presidential election will not be about critical issues but rather a referendum on whether to allow Biden to put his political rival behind bars. The result will almost certainly be a Trump landslide.

There are simply far too many Americans on both sides of the political aisle increasingly angered with Biden's election interference. This is particularly true as inflation rages, our borders crumble, and Communist China, Imperial Russia, the Mullahs of Iran, and North Korea's "Rocket Man" now rise like a bad blood moon.

Let's, however, do more than pray for a landslide. Let's get out there and make it happen so that Donald Trump can be our forty-seventh president and de-weaponize our court system.

CHAPTER 19

Defending Our Constitutional Judiciary

by Mike Davis, founder and president, Article III Project (A3P)

In President Trump's first term, he achieved an extraordinary feat: the reshaping of the Supreme Court and the pivotal thirteen appellate courts throughout the United States.

President Trump's historic appointments began with the placement of Justice Neil Gorsuch into the position left by Justice Scalia. This was swiftly followed by the appointment of Justice Brett Kavanaugh in place of Justice Kennedy, and, finally, the Supreme Court saw its first constitutionalist majority in nearly a century with the replacement of the late Justice Ruth Bader Ginsburg by Justice Amy Coney Barrett.

Trump's appointments revolutionized the Supreme Court, transforming it from a 5-4 Left-leaning court to a 5-4 conservative Clarence Thomas court. Without these essential shifts, the unchecked power of the federal government, particularly the administrative state, would be a dangerous reality.

Underpinning these decisions is a vital constitutional concern: In our federal system, it should be Congress's duty to enact laws, the president's role to enforce them, and the responsibility of the courts to interpret and apply these laws.

This delicate balance between the federal government and the states, and the equilibrium among the three coequal branches of the federal government, is designed to shield us, the citizens, from an overpowering federal government. This underscores the critical importance of President Trump's transformation of the federal judiciary during his first term.

However, this crucial transformation has been largely undone by President Joe Biden. A second Biden term will not only tilt the courts of appeals to the Left but also risk the loss of the Clarence Thomas court.

Biden's sole criterion for nominating judges appears to be picking Left-leaning candidates based on their race or gender rather than their legal competence. This approach is not tenable. It is clear that ethnicity and gender are among the least relevant qualifications for selecting our judiciary's future leaders.

What's more, today's Democrats are no longer liberals who love America and merely differ with conservatives on the best course. They are, in reality, Marxists, radicals, and social justice warriors who despise America. They disregard free speech, uphold censorship, reject objective scientific truths, and are quick to pass judgment in the court of public opinion rather than uphold due process and equal protection under the law. Their approach has politicized and weaponized our justice system.

This leftist fanaticism became glaringly apparent following the Dobbs decision, which overturned *Roe v. Wade*, returning abortion regulations to state jurisdiction. In response, Senate Majority Leader Chuck Schumer all but threatened the lives of justices Kavanaugh and Gorsuch, a clear indication of leftist fascism.

Moreover, the Biden White House and Department of Justice have been encouraging unlawful campaigns of obstruction outside the homes of the six conservative Supreme Court justices for more than a year. These justices and their families were forced to relocate to safe houses due to these threats.

Furthermore, information regarding the Dobbs decision was leaked before its official release. This act, likely intended to undermine the court, has gone unpunished. President Trump will ensure that justice is served.

Appointing constitutionalist federal judges has consistently proven a winning political strategy for conservatives. It played a significant role in President Trump's victory over Hillary Clinton in 2016 and was a contributing factor in the early retirements of at least three Senate Democrats—North Dakota's Heidi Heitkamp, Indiana's Joe Donnelly, and Florida's Bill Nelson—due to their dubious behavior during Justice Brett Kavanaugh's Supreme Court confirmation.

Currently, while a conservative majority holds the Supreme Court, this majority is tenuous and subject to the whims of election results. A reelected President Biden, backed by a Democrat Senate majority, could replace justices Thomas and Alito with

Left-leaning judicial activists. This would turn the 5-4 Clarence Thomas court into a 5-4 Ketanji Brown Jackson court or worse.

Loss of the court would put our fundamental rights—to worship, speak, associate, and protect ourselves—under relentless attack. Through such assaults, we risk losing both our country and our way of life.

Elections do matter. Donald Trump understands that judges matter. On the first day of his second term, President Trump will be prepared with fully vetted, conservative judges to be nominated, and his strategic communications team will be ready to defend all nominees against what will undoubtedly be tough confirmation battles. We must rally to his side in this crucial fight.

CHAPTER 20

Freeing the J6 Prisoners

Violence of any kind—particularly against law enforcement officers—should never be condoned. President Trump emphasized this throughout his first term, and he will continue to do so.

However, *lawfare* waged against Americans by a weaponized judicial system based on political or religious affiliation runs counter to every democratic principle our republic was founded upon.

During the January 6, 2021, protest of the 2020 presidential election—which was riddled with all manner of fraud and irregularities—the vast majority of Americans came to Washington, D.C., to protest peacefully. It now appears, however, that much of the "J6" violence that ensued on Capitol Hill was instigated not by Trump supporters, but rather by *agent provocateurs*—including FBI informants—seeking to block the efforts of President Trump to peacefully get a legal counting of the vote. This J6 violence was also apparently facilitated by Capitol Hill police officers, some of whom removed barriers and waved protesters into what we now know was an entrapment scheme.

Rather than conduct a full investigation, the Biden regime has sought to exploit the J6 violence to brand President Trump as an insurrectionist and "legal terrorist." Their obvious partisan purpose was to prevent him from running for president again—or at least wound Trump politically.

Congress's Kangaroo Court "investigation" of J6, orchestrated by a pack of Never-Trump jackals, featured only one-sided testimony from President Trump's political enemies and selective and heavily edited video from inside the Capitol. This investigation also failed to answer why Democrat House Speaker Nancy Pelosi rejected the ten thousand National Guard troops requested by President Trump leading up to J6; why lethal force was *unnecessarily* used against Marine veteran Ashli Babbitt; why Rosanne Boyland was beaten to death by Capitol Police; why Capitol Police freely opened doors for protestors; and why as many as forty FBI informants were present at the protest.

In the aftermath of this instigated violence, Biden's DOJ illegally denied the J6 defendants fair trials by subjecting them to biased federal judges and heavily Democrat-skewed jury pools. In April 2022, a poll was conducted by Inlux Research and Analytics that revealed that more than 90 percent of D.C. jurors maintained preconceived biases against J6 defendants before trial.

Of equal note, the Chief Judge of the D.C. circuit, Beryl Howell—an Obama appointment—openly told a J6 defendant and jury *in court* that the results of the 2020 election should not be questioned.

Because J6 was the "crime of the century," she believed non-violent J6 protestors should be given much harsher punishments.

Today, the J6 prisoners—many of whom are military veterans—continue to be denied their constitutional rights inside federal prison. In violation of the First Amendment and the Religious Land Use and Institutionalized Persons Act (RLIUPA), J6 defendants have been denied access to religious visits or services and Holy Communion.

In violation of the Sixth and Eighth amendments, many J6 defendants have been denied bail, kept in lengthy pretrial detention, and spent up to nineteen months in solitary confinement.

That's nearly forty times longer than the international standard adopted by the United Nations.

On top of this, some J6 prisoners have even been driven to suicide as a result, while cancer-ridden J6 defendants like Chris Worrell have been denied access to doctors while in pretrial detention.

The Biden regime's relentless, partisan pursuit of Trump loyalists is in sharp contrast to that of the government's response to *far worse abuses* by violent extremists and agitators on the Left. Consider that during the Black Lives Matter (BLM) riots of 2020, which resulted in $2 billion in property damages nationwide, demolished minority-owned businesses, and caused nearly thirty American deaths, charges were dropped on 90 percent of the perpetrators. This is in sharp contrast to the staggering 98 percent conviction rate for J6 cases.

Among the three hundred DOJ-indicted BLM rioters, at least thirty-two of the thirty-nine individuals charged with "assaulting a federal officer" had their cases dismissed. This included Jason

Correa, who ran at federal officers multiple times with a shield and kicked them repeatedly.

In sharp contrast, J6 defendant and former deputy sheriff Colt McAbee, who was also charged with assault for attempting to stop Capitol Police from beating unarmed Rosanne Boyland to death on video and even protected police officers from the crowd, awaits a potential maximum sentence of decades in jail.

Add all this tyranny and torture up, and it is clear that the Biden regime has not pursued justice but has simply administered partisan retribution. Accordingly, on his first day in office, President Trump will graciously grant pardons and reduced sentences on a case-by-case basis for all Americans unfairly charged with crimes they never committed, experienced disparate treatment by a biased DOJ, or been subjected to forms of cruel and unusual punishment in relation to J6.

President Trump should also order his own DOJ to conduct a full and proper investigation. This will include an investigation of the FBI itself for its apparently complicit role in a malicious and partisan entrapment scheme.

CHAPTER 21

Ensuring Free, Honest, and Fair Elections and Election Integrity

Free, fair, and secure elections represent the most fundamental principles of maintaining a strong democracy and republic. Election integrity is not just a God-given and constitutional right; it is a national security issue. This is especially true when lives are at stake, for example, when we must choose the right president to combat Chinese Communist aggression, secure our borders against an invasion of illegal immigrants, contain a revanchist Russia, or battle foreign terrorist threats like Iran, Al Qaeda, and North Korea.

In the 2020 presidential race, Joe Biden was declared the winner amid great controversy. Elections do indeed have consequences and stolen elections have catastrophic consequences. This illegitimate president promptly began failing this nation on Communist China, Afghanistan, our southern border, Ukraine, our now stagflationary economy, racism and pedophilia in our schools, and the containment of terrorism.

Today, there is a growing consensus that America would be far better off if Trump had been declared the winner, as many believe quite reasonably that he should have been. It's not for nothing that a supermajority of Republicans and nearly half of the American people believe the 2020 presidential race was rigged.

The three-volume Navarro Report, published just months after the November 2020 election, remains the most comprehensive report published to date on the alleged fraud and election irregularities. This report, endorsed by Donald Trump, consolidated reams of evidence of potential voter fraud from the Trump campaign, legal experts, and volunteers. The research included a review of more than fifty lawsuits and judicial rulings, thousands of affidavits and declarations, public testimony in state venues, public analyses by think tanks and legal centers, and more.

The central finding of the Navarro Report is that the Democrats used a "grand stuff-the-ballot-box strategy" executed through both legal and illegal means. This strategy was deployed nationwide but used with particular effectiveness to tip the election in Joe Biden's favor by targeting the six battleground states of Arizona, Georgia, Nevada, Michigan, Pennsylvania, and Wisconsin.

As one part of its strategic pincer movement, the Democrats drastically *increased* the flood of absentee and mail-in ballots—the types of ballots most susceptible to election fraud. The Democrats then gamed the rules of the system to drastically *decrease* the level of scrutiny of these mail-in ballots through reducing ID requirements—i.e., relaxed signature-matching—and automatic and same-day voter registration, thereby making it far easier for illegal ballots to be counted.

As an example of a *legal* tactic designed to increase the flow of *illegal* ballots, Nevada's state legislature passed AB-4 just months before the 2020 election day. It legalized state-wide universal mail-in ballots, ballot harvesting, ballot receipt deadline extensions, ballot curing extensions, and relaxed signature-matching verification, *all* in one omnibus bill.

Similarly, in Michigan, the Never-Trumper and anti-MAGA George Soros's Promote the Vote spent $2.5 million collecting signatures during the 2018 midterm elections to change election law in the Michigan Constitution by 2020. This resulted in automatic voter registration, same-day voter registration, no-excuse absentee voting, and extended mail-in voter registration.

On the *illegal* front, Pennsylvania secretary of state Kathy Boockvar—elected with the help of Soros money—*illegally* issued guidance that directed election officials *not* to perform signature matching analysis on absentee and mail-in ballots. This was a clear violation of Pennsylvania's Constitution; it would mean 2020 mail-in ballots would *not* be rejected if signature-match requirements were not valid. The result: Michigan had no proper voter ID checks and Trump got sandbagged.

In addition, Facebook oligarch Mark Zuckerberg poured nearly *half a billion dollars* into local election administration offices. This partisan Never-Trump spending was illegally laundered through a non-profit and used to conduct illegal ballot harvesting operations like "Democracy in the Park" in Wisconsin and boost voter turnout in largely Democrat cities like Philadelphia.

Zuckerberg wound up spending more in the battleground states than the Trump campaign did!

These examples of the two-pronged Democrat strategy listed above are merely a brief overview of what occurred in 2020. They do not include the numerous Democratic party court interventions, extensive propaganda campaigns, process fouls, voting machine irregularities, Equal Protection Clause violations, reduced poll watching and observing during ballot-counting, and much more—as featured in the damning indictment films of Citizens United's *Rigged* and Dinesh D'Souza's *2000 Mules*.

To put the resultant flood of Democrat and illegal ballots in perspective, absentee and mail-in ballots cast during the 2020 election surpassed total absentee and mail-in ballots cast in both the 2016 and 2012 presidential elections *combined*.

When President Trump called for an investigation into the 2020 election, it was never about just overturning election results. President Trump and his MAGA-deplorable base just wanted answers to questions half of the country had about anomalies that arose during the 2020 election to preserve the integrity of our republic.

Regrettably, virtually all of the claims of a rigged election have gone largely uninvestigated and been ignored by the courts. As a consequence, the Democrats—in tacit collusion with the mainstream media—have successfully branded President Trump and anyone else who dared to *question* the legitimacy of the Biden-Harris "win" as insurrectionists or "election deniers."

Adding dangerous insult to this injury to our republic, a weaponized Biden "Department of Injustice" continues to aggressively seek to put many of those who have challenged the election results behind bars using Obama-appointed judges and biased jury pools as their tools. When President Trump wins his *third* election in 2024, he will appoint a true MAGA Republican as attorney general rather than a RINO like Bill Barr.

Barr not only suppressed the Hunter Biden laptop story and thereby helped rig the election—polls clearly indicate that if voters had known the contents of that laptop, they would have swung heavily to Trump. The RINO Barr also refused to promptly and properly investigate the November 2020 election. Trump's new attorney general will get to the bottom of the irregularities as well as cease the weaponization of both the FBI and the DOJ.

- To ensure a proper, bipartisan investigation—as opposed to the Kangaroo Court established by Nancy Pelosi with her "select committee"—President Trump should also promptly appoint a bipartisan Presidential Commission on Election Integrity to conduct a *full* and *proper* investigation into what exactly happened on November 3, 2020.
- President Trump will also ban voting procedures for future presidential elections that lead to election *insecurity*, and mandate election measures that lead to election *security*.

This order will ban unsupervised ballot drop boxes, ballot harvesting, universal mail-in ballots, corruptible and hackable electronic voting machine systems, and private money influencing, mandate robust voter ID laws, and establish a national holiday to allow one-day voting.

President Trump believes we must look forward to ensuring election integrity, but we also must remember the frauds of the past. Otherwise, America will be compelled to repeat them.

CHAPTER 22

Eradicating Forced Vaccinations and Holding Mainstream Media Liable for Deadly Misreporting

by Dr. Steven Hatfill, medical adviser to the Defense Production Act Policy Coordinator, Trump Administration

In the 1950s, President Eisenhower issued a warning to Americans about the dangers of an unjustified influence exerted by the U.S. military-industrial complex. This concept referred to an interconnected network of interests, commonly known as the "iron triangle," in which Congress passed legislation favoring defense contractors who, in turn, provided support for reelection campaigns. These contractors would then lobby Congress on behalf of the U.S. military, resulting in special treatment for themselves. Ultimately, the bureaucracy frequently received increased funding to administer federal policies.

Recently, the COVID-19 pandemic has exposed a second and more sinister variant of the iron triangle that has remained concealed within the federal bureaucracy for the past three decades. This insidious entity takes the form of the "Big Pharma–federal health agency industrial complex," which has now come to light due to relentless Freedom of Information Act (FOIA) requests and lawsuits filed by organizations like Judicial Watch and America's First Legal.

Throughout the COVID-19 pandemic, the CDC, the NIH, and the FDA have repeatedly assured all Americans that the COVID-19 mRNA "vaccines" were highly effective, well-tested, and completely safe. In actuality, the mRNA vaccines have never been safe, effective, or completely tested.

Before any new FDA approval, pharmacokinetic studies are necessary to establish product efficacy and safety in humans. Yet FOIA documents recovered by Judicial Watch show that no absorption studies, no metabolism studies, no excretion studies, and no pharmacokinetic studies were ever conducted with the Moderna experimental mRNA 1273 COVID-19 vaccine. We also now know that Pfizer never released all of its animal testing data after the FDA issued it an Emergency Use Authorization (EUA).

A Japanese government lawsuit forced the release of Pfizer's biodistribution study, which showed that the mRNA vaccines did not remain localized upon injection but instead quickly spread throughout many tissues. We now know that the vaccine mRNA can stay active in the body for days if not weeks.

We also know that repeated vaccination with mRNA boosters can lead to toxic viral spike protein damage to the human liver, heart, testes, ovaries, and spleen, with widespread damage to the microcirculation and the deposition of the abnormal spike protein amyloid in the brains of repeated vaccine/booster recipients. This abnormal amyloid deposition is accompanied by biomarkers of neurodegeneration formerly associated with Alzheimer's, the Parkinson's disease spectrum, and dementia. The long-term effects of this are unknown at this time.

In addition, further FOIA documents show that a "statistically significant" number of baby rats were born with skeletal deformations after their mothers were injected with the Moderna vaccine. The FDA has dismissed this animal data, saying that the skeletal anomalies were "not considered adverse." However, leading experts in this field agree that *the highly experimental mRNA "vaccines" should never have been authorized for use during pregnancy*. Lax and inaccurate vaccine adverse event surveillance makes the true incidence of human miscarriages associated with the mRNA vaccines uncertain.

FOIA records also detail internal discussions about mRNA vaccine-induced heart inflammation (myocarditis). Publicly, the CDC and FDA have tried to downplay this serious event. However, leading cardiologists maintain that all cases of myocarditis are serious. *The mRNA vaccines should never have been authorized for young adults, children, and babies who lack any benefit–risk ratio.*

In late 2020, the Brighton Collaboration created a priority list of adverse events that should be assessed for the COVID-19 mRNA vaccines. In 2022, a small group of prominent clinical data scientists used this list to reanalyze the placebo-controlled, phase III randomized clinical trials of the Pfizer and Moderna mRNA COVID-19 "vaccines" in adults (clinical trials NCT04368728 and NCT04470427). This reanalyzed manufacturer clinical trial data clearly demonstrates a negative benefit-to-risk ratio in individuals who took the Moderna or Pfizer mRNA COVID-19 "vaccines."

The injected mRNA "vaccine" instructs the body to produce a highly toxic, harmful molecule called the spike protein for weeks after injection. Both the Moderna and Pfizer manufacturer's clinical trials show these mRNA vaccines cause a higher risk of post-vaccine hospitalization, disability, and a life-changing event that is *greater than the risk of being unvaccinated and* naturally catching a COVID-19 infection and being hospitalized with it. These mRNA products should never have been given to humans.

Instead of an immediate halt to mRNA mass vaccination in January 2022, the program continued to run, poorly supervised, for another sixteen months until the pandemic emergency ended.

Throughout 2021, 2022, and 2023, a majority of the American population has essentially served as uninformed, often coerced or mandated medical test subjects for the ineffective, poorly tested, unsafe, and highly experimental mRNA COVID-19 "pseudo-vaccines."

This coercion violated the 1947 Nuremberg Code, which provided ethical guidelines for human research, the later 1964 Declaration of Helsinki that reaffirmed the need for informed consent in human research, the 1978 Belmont Report that framed these issues into "broader" ethical principles, and the International Covenant on Civil and Political Rights (ICCPR), which provides that "no one shall be subjected without his free consent to medical or scientific experimentation."

During the U.S. mass vaccination program, the highly experimental COVID-19 mRNA vaccines were administered without informed consent. Even worse, all federal employees, the U.S. military, healthcare workers, students, and airline pilots were mandated to receive the problematic vaccines with repeated federal health agency recommendations for the vaccination of young adults, children, and infants. *These were groups without any demonstrable benefit-to-risk ratio.*

As observed with the mRNA vaccine debacle, in spite of international agreements outlining ethical guidelines for human experimentation, *there is still a need for a definitive, legal, enforceable norm to protect the rights of all Americans against experimental vaccine mandates.* As of this writing, the American people have little to no trust in the federal health agencies.

President Trump will restore this trust through urgent action.

Recent FOIA documents obtained by America First Legal clearly outline that the CDC was actively suppressing the free speech of U.S. citizens on the social media platforms of Twitter, Facebook, and Instagram, intentionally blocking and actively deplatforming highly educated physicians and scientists who were trying to warn the public of the proven safety and effectiveness of hydroxychloroquine and Ivermectin as early outpatient treatments for COVID- 19 and the dangers of the experimental mass mRNA vaccination program.

- By executive order, President Trump should explicitly prohibit all federal agencies from interfering with the practice of medicine and the freedom of speech exercised by doctors and scientists on social media platforms or any other public "town hall" communications.
- President Trump should immediately put into place mechanisms to hold the commercial mainstream media accountable for any prolonged and incorrect reporting on medical topics

that result in injury or death. This accountability will help safeguard the public from misinformation and ensure that accurate and reliable information is disseminated. Liability measures with no statute of limitations should be the consequences for spreading false or misleading medical information.

In the face of the overwhelming statistics, the histologically proven vaccine tissue damage, and the lack of efficacy, the Biden vaccination mandates severely tested the U.S. Constitution and Bill of Rights. Technically, many state governors, schools, universities, hospitals, companies, and corporations all violated international ethics considerations by coercing and subjecting their state residents to experimental medical procedures [sic, mRNA vaccines] that for months carried a significant demonstrable risk without any benefit.

- By executive order, President Trump should immediately roll back all forced vaccination policies and ban medical coercion and mandates for medical treatments and procedures. This will protect individuals' rights to make autonomous decisions about their own healthcare and prevent undue pressure or force to undergo medical interventions.
- President Trump should also propose an amendment to the Bill of Rights that explicitly requires fully informed consent for all clinical trial participants and the general public.

The carnage caused by Anthony Fauci, individual companies like Pfizer, and, most broadly, the Big Pharma–federal health agency industrial complex must never be allowed to happen again.

CHAPTER 23

Cleaning DEI out of Academia

Including everyone who desires to participate in America's educational process and prohibiting discrimination against students or faculty based on their demographics is something you would think that all Americans had come to agree on. In the 1950s, Republican president Dwight D. Eisenhower sent troops into the South to open public schools to Black students and to protect Blacks from the exploitation at the hands of racist Democratic politicians and their KKK allies. Eventually, young Northern liberals joined the fight against Jim Crow as well. However, after the important battles of the civil rights era were settled, the activists from the Left simply could not give up fighting for fighting's sake. Pushing the boundaries of government deeper into American society had become their raison d'être.

In the realm of diversity and inclusion, the Left quietly moved from arguing for *equality of opportunity* to *equity of outcomes.* Defining the "E" in DEI as "equity" is a matter of the largest consequence. DEI proponents believe that it is up to the government to ensure the success of each and every minority candidate, regardless of individual talent, motivation, or results, and to prioritize guaranteed success based on a dizzying and constantly evolving taxonomy of race and gender. This taxonomy is clearly designed to exclude their political opponents from academic and economic opportunity. The progressive Left sees people not as equal citizens with different skills and ambitions, but as objects defined entirely by their racial and gender identities.

In 1996, the wise voters of the Golden State passed proposition 209, a law modeled on the 1964 Civil Rights Act. It amended the state constitution to prohibit state governmental institutions from considering race, sex, or ethnicity in hiring, contracting, and education. Every candidate would have to stand on his or her own merits and could not be excluded based on the color of their skin or their sexual equipment. Similar anti-discrimination laws were promulgated in other states and upheld by the United States Supreme Court in 2014. Again, almost every American agreed this made sense. Polls consistently show Americans do not support racial or gender discrimination. A 2023 Pew survey asked Americans if they approved of "selective colleges and universities taking race and ethnicity into account in admissions decisions in order to increase the racial and ethnic diversity at the school." Half opposed this racial pandering, while only a third supported it.

Still our leftist intellectual elites, being sure that they are entitled to rule over the average Americans—whom they will routinely despise and mock in closed academic settings—were determined to find legal work-arounds that would let them continue with "affirmative action."

Valuing this caste system above all else, they moved to enforce it regardless of the cost to once highly respected institutions from Harvard to the University of California.

Needing a way to categorize faculty based on their identity caste system, they instituted a new requirement in hiring process, known as the "Diversity Statement." These written statements became required elements of job applications at many universities, public and private. They require the writer applicant to discuss their experiences with racial and gender discrimination and work they have done on the topic. "People of color," women, gays, and the ever-growing panoply of newly defined genders are essentially assured success as they can assert having experienced discrimination firsthand. White males find themselves forced to argue that they have been "fellow travelers," working alongside their poor, disenfranchised peers as activists and producing a Maoist "self-criticism" statement. They must curse their fate having been born of European descent and with testicles. They must denounce their parents and ancestors for supposedly ruining everything in human history.

This tactic has worked beautifully in excluding white males from opportunities they would otherwise win based on merit and packing universities with faculty who fit nicely into slots on the intersectional rainbow flag. On September 8, the *New York Times* reported, "At Berkeley, a faculty committee rejected 75 percent of applicants in life sciences and environmental sciences and management purely on diversity statements." A 2023 research paper by Steven Brint and Komi Frey showed the power of the diversity statement to discriminate against whites at the UC campus. While Hispanics made up just 13 percent of applicants for faculty positions, they made up 59 percent of the post-diversity statement finalists. Whites who made up 54 percent of the applicants were reduced to just 14 percent of the finalists.

These statements are also used to eliminate Asian candidates, whose astounding success is due to cultural respect for education and hard work. The liberal elites despise those "tiger mom" characteristics and see Asians as entitled and their high standards as intolerant. Asian American candidates at Berkeley dropped from 25 percent of applicants to just 18 percent of finalists after being "diversity filtered."

To discourage white faculty members from continuing in education or seeking advancement they are often subjected to formal diversity sensitivity and training sessions or simply random bouts of public humiliation where they are ridiculed for their role in the infamous "white male patriarchy." The political angle to this cannot be missed and these meetings often include anti-Republican rhetoric as well. Zack DePiero, an English professor at Penn State, reported that his direct supervisor shared, in front of colleagues, her "horror" upon discovering that DePiero "was not a registered Democrat."

The strategy for keeping white and Asian students out of our universities has centered around test scores. Arguing that things like English grammar and trigonometry are racist, the state of California removed test scores as admissions and scholarship criteria starting in 2022. The result will be that only high school grades and admissions essays will matter. The grade ranking will treat all high schools as equally rigorous, which they clearly are not. The essays will allow the admissions team to make the racial and gender-based choices they want. This system also disenfranchises those pesky home-schooled kids, who are known to be disproportionately white.

Sadly, all students are not the same. Some extremely bright students, minority kids in particular, are bored by their weak high school curriculum or distracted by an increasingly dangerous environment. While their grades are mediocre, these students have often been rescued by their SAT or ACT scores. In fact, the University of California recognized this reality and used to have a special clause that would ignore grades and admit some students purely on test scores. The new system must warm the hearts of the academic bureaucrats because it excludes the sort of creative and disruptive thinkers who would challenge their beloved caste system.

The second Trump administration will eliminate all of these manufactured systems for enforcing the Left's discriminatory agenda. Universities that utilize diversity statements, ignore test scores, or contrive other novel hiring and admission mechanisms with the intent of evading anti-discrimination laws will be denied federal funding. American educators and students will be evaluated on their aptitude and efforts and nothing else.

CHAPTER 24

Donald Trump Will Hold Communist China and Anthony Fauci Accountable for COVID-19

The Chinese Communist virus known as COVID-19 not only killed millions of people worldwide and inflicted trillions of dollars of damages on the U.S. economy. It also spawned the greatest hoax in world medical history, namely, that this deadly, genetically engineered virus spawned in a bioweapons lab in Wuhan, China, came from nature.

The Chinese Communist Party *spawned* this "wet market," natural origin hoax because it did not want to be blamed for the chaos, death, and damages it knew the virus and ensuing pandemic would inflict on this world. To spawn this hoax, the CCP ordered the destruction of evidence at the Wuhan Institute of Virology that would have immediately proven the virus was from this bioweapons lab, even as it similarly destroyed evidence at a Wuhan wet market that would have proved the virus was clearly not from nature.

The CCP also significantly pressured the World Health Organization to support the "comes from nature" theory. The CCP's WHO puppets would dutifully issue communications and a report in support of that absurdity, with great impact on world opinion.

Public health bureaucrats in Washington, D.C., led by doctors Anthony Fauci and Francis Collins, helped *perpetuate* this hoax because they did not want to take any responsibility for all of the blood that was really dripping from their hands. As we would subsequently learn, Fauci and Collins themselves did an end run around the Trump administration to resume so-called "gain of function" research at the Wuhan lab.

By transferring gain of function technology to Communist China and by using American taxpayer money to fund the Wuhan bioweapons lab, Fauci and Collins effectively taught their Chinese Communist counterparts how to genetically engineer deadly viruses. When news began to break of a mysterious deadly virus appearing in Wuhan in December 2019, Fauci and Collins knew full well that their research funding might turn out to be the root source of the pandemic.

To inoculate themselves from any criticism, Fauci and Collins recruited a group of scientists that had received funding from his bureaucracy to help engineer a cover-up, including most prominently Dr. Kristian Andersen of Scripps Research and Dr. Robert Garry of Tulane. To this end, Fauci and Collins held a conference call in February 2020 with these scientists.

While the scientists initially leaned toward the lab theory on the call, they quickly switched their position and began drafting a research paper that would appear in the prestigious *Nature Medicine* journal under the headline "The Proximal Origin of SARS-CoV-2"

(COVID-19). In that article, with the fingerprints of neither Fauci nor Collins visible, these scientists gave a full- throated defense of the natural origin theory; Andersen and Collins would later receive approval for an $8.9 million grant proposal that was pending with Fauci at the time of the conference call.

During President Trump's second term, he will get to the bottom of the origins of COVID-19 and ensure that all parties responsible for causing the pandemic and then covering up its origins will be held both financially and criminally accountable for their actions. To that end, President Trump should issue an executive order establishing a presidential commission to investigate the origins of COVID-19 and its subsequent cover-up, estimate the full range of economic damages caused by the pandemic to the U.S. economy, and make recommendations as to how to recover the costs of any such damages through appropriate reparations.

The Trump COVID-19 commission could be modeled after previous presidential commissions that have investigated national tragedies, from the Japanese attack on Pearl Harbor and the Kennedy assassination to the BP Deepwater Horizon oil spill. This commission will be staffed by a prestigious group of virologists and bio-weapons experts and economists and co-chaired by a Senate and House member.

Note that estimating the far-reaching economic costs of the pandemic will require considerable economic expertise to parse what may well be the most complex "general equilibrium" problem America has ever faced. General equilibrium analysis focuses on how changes in one or more (partial equilibrium) markets of an economy might ripple through the broader macroeconomy and financial markets.

For example, Osama bin Laden's 9/11 attack was an isolated attack on the Twin Towers of the World Trade Center and on the Pentagon. However, this attack would lead to two lengthy wars and dramatic and far-reaching structural changes in our economy—deadly stones in an American pond catalyzing a tsunami of destructive economic ripples and waves.

COVID-19 has wrought similar, and arguably even more complex, structural changes in our economy, which we are still sorting out. As just one example, the commercial real estate sector in the United States is now on life support as "work from home" habits learned in the pandemic have hollowed out urban landscapes across America and led to unprecedented vacancy rates and bankruptcies.

Meanwhile, the United States continues to run massive budget deficits, equally unprecedented in our history. Much of this deficit spending is the result of myriad responses to the pandemic.

All such economic costs—including the loss of life—must and will be accounted for. As the "ultimate tort," these costs will be aggressively recovered through reparations from the perpetrator, with such costs likely to be found to be as high as an entire year's gross domestic product of this country—well north of $20 trillion.

In a parallel effort, President Trump should use his constitutional authority to direct the Justice Department and Federal Bureau of Investigation to fully investigate the roles of doctors Anthony Fauci and Francis Collins and any research scientists Fauci and Collins may have engaged with to perpetuate the wet market hoax. President Trump will ensure that if Fauci and Collins and their co-conspirators have indeed engaged in a cover-up, they will be prosecuted to the full extent of the law and be held legally liable for any costs they helped inflict.

CHAPTER 25

Reading, Writing, and Arithmetic–
Not Wokeness in School Curricula

The Greek philosopher Diogenes, who was known for his brutal honesty, notes that "the foundation of every state is the education of its youth." Instead of reading, writing, and arithmetic, students in America are now being taught pornography and perversion, to hate their country, and that the imperfections of our founding fathers far outweigh their heroism and brilliance in defeating tyranny to establish the greatest country in the world.

Of course, the more our schools indoctrinate our children and young adults with distorted facts, disfigured history, deviant sexual behavior such as pedophilia, and false motives behind the founding of our country, the more our people will engage in abhorrent behavior, grow disunified, and our culture and society will erode.

As you read this, radical woke teachers on the Biden Left are pedaling literal porn, LGBTQ propaganda, and even pedophilia to underage children and young high school and college students. Indeed, parents are being forced to send their kids as young as eleven to be taught lessons on anal sex by adult male cross-dressers, study textbooks on ten-year-old boys performing oral sex on each other, and read about young boys engaging in gay sex with full-grown men.

You can't make that up. It is real, it is increasingly ubiquitous, it is abhorrent, and it is perverting our young children at the most impressionable time in their lives. And it is Joe Biden, Vice-President Kamala Harris, and Biden's attorney general that are providing the enforcement mechanism for such perversion.

That's right. If you are a parent who shows up rightfully angry at a school board meeting to object, you may well be deemed a domestic terrorist by the Biden regime's Department of (In)Justice. It has happened many times before, and it will happen again until Donald Trump and an angry coalition of parents boot the Bidenites out of the White House temple.

Unfortunately, the Biden regime is not just pedaling perversion in our schools. It is also making great strides in turning our children away from their American roots and identity. Polls now indicate that only a small fraction of Americans under age thirty see patriotism as being very important to them.

Lack of pride in the USA in turn means fewer Americans committed to upholding our founding principles in roles of public service—or wanting to serve in general. Writ large, this is a grave national security risk.

Just look at our military, which faces one of the greatest recruitment crises in history. Aside from the fact that many young

Americans are disqualified from joining due to rising mental health problems and obesity—another problem in itself—91 percent of qualified young Americans have *zero* interest in joining in the first place. Compare that to the baby boomer generation, who were *six times* as likely to have served in the military.

This antipathy to defending our country comes as no surprise when our education system embraces toxic ideologies, like Critical Race Theory, which oppose American values. CRT is now as toxic as it is increasingly ubiquitous.

Astonishingly, CRT has been adopted in universities across all fifty states—including medical schools. Yet, CRT was developed to Americanize a 1930s Marxist theory. In this Karl Marx reboot, "morality" is a fluid and godless concept that should be based on what caters to the interest of oppressed groups. In the name of this new CRT morality, these groups should overthrow the ruling class by dismantling all societal norms such as family, capitalism, and God.

Importantly, instead of focusing on socio-economic class struggle like the Communist Marx, CRT focuses on race—specifically, white people—as the main oppressors of Black Americans. Through the racist lens of CRT, those with white skin should acknowledge their "privilege," confess their guilt, and pay for the sins of their ancestors through instruments such as reparations and affirmative action–type programs that push "white folk" out.

What is perhaps most offensive about all of this is that CRT ignores the great strides America has made in addressing race relations, particularly since the beginning of the Civil Rights Movement. Instead, CRT teaches students across America that the same level of oppression still occurs today as at the founding of our republic, that Black Americans are perpetual victims of a white society and are incapable of accomplishing anything without their help, and that white people are inherently superior and endlessly indebted to Black Americans.

Given such indoctrination—and the increasingly racist and ironic rhetoric of a supposedly woke Left—it's no surprise that 80 percent of college freshmen believe America is racist. Nor should it be surprising that an increasing number of America's students graduate from college hating God and family and wanting to dismantle our country.

The poster child for all of this CRT racism and anti-Americanism is the domestic terrorist group Black Lives Matter (BLM). BLM's role in the 2020 riots led to billions in property damages, minority-owned businesses demolished, and dozens of American deaths, including law enforcement officers and children. Yet today, BLM proudly lives out this CRT–Marxist ideology. Not surprisingly, their most active participants are young Americans aged eighteen to thirty-four.

Failing to identify and challenge this corruption within our education system will create further division in our country, less willingness to engage in public service, and lead our children to believe things about reality or themselves that aren't true—for example, that white people are endlessly in debt to Black people, or that men can become women.

Donald Trump understands these problems and he will act swiftly to turn our schools away from perversion and propaganda and back to a world in which our schools teach basic skills like reading, writing, and arithmetic while preparing students for an increasingly competitive world.

To rid our society of wokeness in our schools, he should direct all schools that receive federal funding to

- Incorporate a daily recitation of the Pledge of Allegiance.
- Provide mandatory coursework on American history, constitutional values, our founding principles, and the dangers of socialism and communism.
- Completely ban from their curricula CRT, pornographic, and LGBTQ materials.

In November 2020, President Trump signed an executive order to establish the 1776 Presidential Commission to help students across America better understand the founding principles of our nation to form a more perfect union. This executive order mandated federal agencies to use their resources to promote patriotic education and tasked the commission with writing a report on how our nation's principles should be taught and celebrated in school. In President Trump's second term, he will also likely reinstate this executive order.

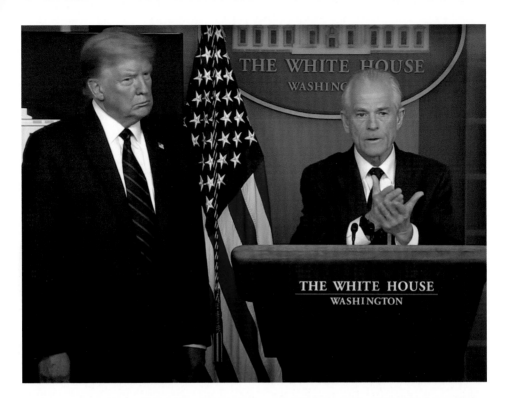

Here I am addressing the press in my role as Policy Coordinator of the National Defense Production Act. President Donald J. Trump acted decisively to deliver the materials our industrial base sorely needed.

All photographs courtesy of the Donald J. Trump Presidential Library

President Trump signs an executive order withdrawing the U.S. from the Trans-Pacific Partnership (TPP). The TPP would have sent more American jobs overseas and cheapened our economy. I applauded our swift withdrawal from the partnership.

Nobody stood up to China like President Donald J. Trump. The Chinese took advantage of the United States for far too long. President Trump put a stop to this abuse.

The revival of American industry was one of the Trump administration's greatest achievements, and one in which I was proud to play a role.

America sorely needs a president who prioritizes our economy and workers. America First means looking out for our interests!

It will take work, but we can bring our jobs back home to the hardworking Americans who so desperately need them.

Securing our southern border was a first-day priority for President Trump.

Unfortunately, the border has totally disintegrated under Biden's unwatchful eye. The second Trump administration will be handed a much more volatile situation this time around.

Serving your country in the White House is a brief but shining honor. I am grateful for my time spent in President Trump's administration, and all the good it did for our people.

Nobody cut more red tape in the federal bureaucracy than President Trump's administration.

Resecuring our energy independence is critical to the America First agenda.

President Trump has nothing but respect for our veterans, and the feeling is mutual.

Striving to Make America Great Again was the honor of a lifetime.

CHAPTER 26

Protecting Parents' Rights and the Right to Choose Their Children's Schools

Adults have incredible influence over children because children naturally look to them for guidance. Parents, in particular, are given this special commandment by God to teach children and steer them to pursue truth. As Proverbs 22:5 teaches us: "Thorns and snares are on the path of the crooked; those who safeguard their lives will avoid them. Train the young in the way they should go; even when old, they will not swerve from it."

Today, the Left has littered our children's path to a useful education with all manner of thorns and snails. Not only are woke teachers freely inflicting perverted, twisted, and America-hating ideology on children, but parents are also being denied the right to choose the best learning environment for their children.

Our country has been publicly funding education for more

than *sixty* years, yet this has failed us and our children miserably. In the latest surveys, the United States is ranked well below one hundred other countries, with more than half of Americans aged between sixteen and seventy-four reading below a sixth-grade level.

On average, the worst proficiency scores—which are measured in slightly different ways state-by-state—are in history, where by twelfth grade, America's students have a *staggeringly low* 12 percent proficiency level. We must remember here Santayana's admonition that those who do not remember the mistakes of the past are condemned to repeat them.

Over the past several years, the mainstream media and leftist politicians have blamed this decline of proficiency on a shortage of teachers, lack of funding and investment, and the cost of education. Although these problems are partially true, they miss the root of the problem: The government, with its woke edicts and curricula, cannot responsibly educate our kids.

Data from the 1990s clearly shows here that regardless of increases in teachers' salaries and funding, since the beginning of public education funding in the 1960s, just 5 percent of seventeen-year-old high school students can read well enough to understand and use information found in technical materials, literary essays, historical documents, and college-level texts.

Since the 1960s, the government has imposed burdensome personnel rules and regulations on public schools that work contrary to the goals of improved educational performance.

For example, teacher incentives are geared toward teachers rather than improving instruction. Salary requirements are decided by states with no relationship to the educational institution; tenure is determined by the amount of time a teacher spends at an institution rather than their students' performance in the classroom; national-level leftist policies like the Obama administration's Common Core platform have reduced testing standards to make people feel good about themselves rather than encouraging higher achievement; and an aggressive push to reward educational institutions to teach students that America is systemically racist are "reforms" for which our children are paying a heavy price.

The CATO Institute found that school choice improves student standardized test scores by approximately 0.27 standard deviations in reading and 0.15 standard deviations in math. Twenty-five randomized-controlled studies show that school choice improves educational attainment—in other words, higher levels of education completed.

School choice is also extremely popular, especially among minorities. For example, 75 percent of African American parents desire to choose their child's school regardless of geographic boundaries—and 72 percent of Americans nationwide support this as well.

Unfortunately, parents in more than half of the country are unable to send their children to a school outside of the district they live in if a specific learning environment is unsuitable. As an alternative, private schools are extremely expensive—and most families, especially in Joe Biden's economy, simply cannot afford steep tuition costs.

School choice is critical to the education "market." With more choice, schools would have to prove the effectiveness of their education by results, not race inclusivity or leftist propaganda. Not only would national educational proficiency in all subject areas improve, woke ideologies now eroding our educational system and perverting the minds of our children would likely dissipate.

Thanks to school choice in states like New Mexico, a mother with an autistic daughter was able to pick an educational system that worked—and her daughter's learning experience, along with her physical and mental health, greatly improved. On top of this, she was able to access certain services for her daughter that were previously unavailable.

In Oklahoma, a parent complained about the constant switching between online and in-person learning for her children during the CCP virus pandemic, which was highly detrimental to their education. Her son's grades were seriously suffering, until she was able to switch his school system—then, he ended up receiving straight As and enjoyed learning once again.

President Trump believes strongly in school choice. During his first term, he created important opportunities for low-income families to receive educational vouchers to pay for private school tuition. Not only will he reinstate these policies, but Trump as POTUS will also sign an executive order to mandate universal school choice for the entire country.

This executive order will force public schools to employ the highest-quality teachers, enable them to fire those who do not perform well, and incentivize schools to bolster their quality of education to attract families.

Additionally, President Trump has promised financial incentives for schools that develop a parental bill of rights, which would promote curriculum transparency for parents. In turn, schools will rightfully return their focus to reading, writing, and arithmetic rather than LGBTQ, CRT, and slanted race-based U.S. history.

CHAPTER 27

Just Say Double No to Sex-Change Operations for Children

As gender dysphoria surges among America's youth and Biden and the Democrats push for greater and greater accessibility of life-altering medical procedures, our children are now more than ever at risk of mutilation and suicide. This trend is so bizarre and disturbing that President Trump believes he must put an immediate halt to it.

Gender dysphoria is defined as a mental disorder in which one feels their biological sex is misaligned from the gender one identifies with. Those struggling with gender dysphoria typically pursue hormonal therapy and even gender transition surgery—yes, that is what you think it is—to alter the healthy bodies they have been born with to suit the gender of their choice.

The problem, of course, is that gender dysphoria is a fluid concept. While a biologically male child may "feel" at the time he is actually a "she," these feelings can change as the child ages. Fact: Approximately 80 percent of children who identify as gender dysphoric grow out of it when they go through puberty. Too bad for those children whose parents mutilate them only to find out that it was literally a case of mistaken identity.

Despite the horrifying consequences of both gender transition surgery and hormonal therapy, the United States has the most lenient gender transition surgery laws out of even the most progressive countries on the issue. As an example, in virtually *every* European country, gender transition surgery is *illegal* before the age of eighteen, and parental consent is required. In the United States, however, gender transition surgery can be performed on kids as young as twelve years of age.

What's most puzzling about the Biden regime's push for gender transition treatments is that doctors currently have no real idea as to what causes gender dysphoria in the first place. Theories range from the hormones a baby is exposed to in the womb and genetic development, to even cultural and environmental factors.

So, how in the *world* does it make sense to push oftentimes irreversible and life-altering medicine on Americans—especially children—as a sure-fire solution to the disorder they're dealing with? Is it not common sense to first search for the root of a problem in order to properly solve it?

Biden and the Democrats have also branded gender transition medical procedures as "safe and effective" for children. Yes, you've heard that one many times before from our government; it's the go-to propaganda slogan used when typically describing experimental medicine that is actually *not* safe.

A recent poster child for this propaganda is the mRNA "vaccine" for the Communist China virus. In fact, the Fauci jab is not really a vaccine at all but an assault on a child's immune system, which can cause, for example, heart problems in young boys and menstruation issues in young women.

In the case of gender dysphoria, the dangerous hormone therapies now being peddled to parents for their children have been found to result in higher rates of blood clots, strokes, and other forms of cardiovascular mortality.

Sadly, Biden's Department of Health and Human Services (HHS) also falsely claims that gender transition medical procedures are "literally suicide-prevention care." This is simply a grotesque lie as these victims are driven to a suicide rate *twenty times* that of their peers—even a decade after surgery.

Here's the broader science: The human brain finishes development, on average, in a person's mid-to-late twenties. At twelve years of age, the amygdala—which controls reactions including impulse, fear, and aggressive behavior—is more developed than the frontal cortex, which controls reasoning and helps us think before we act. Therefore, twelve-year-olds are more likely to act on impulse and engage in risky behavior. With this in mind, it is clear that neither a twelve-year-old child nor the parent of a twelve-year-old child is capable of consenting to radical and irreversible medical procedures.

Chloe Cole, an anti-gender-transition activist, describes her devastating transgender journey that began at twelve years old. When she first told her parents she felt she was a boy—which she later attributes to incidents of molestation and LGBTQ social media propaganda she was exposed to—her parents had no clue what to do.

Thinking they could rely on doctors for sound medical advice, at thirteen, she was prescribed puberty blockers. By fifteen, she got a double mastectomy to remove her healthy breast tissue. By sixteen, in stark contrast, she regretted it all and quickly halted the process. Her potential future for motherhood had been *eviscerated*, and the doctors who first got her into the mess abandoned her.

In the United States, the rate of children on that very same hormonal therapy has *doubled* from 2,394 in 2017 to 5,063 in 2021. This is madness—until you follow the money!

Big Pharma and its doctors have little incentive to oppose transgender medical treatments. On average, they receive a hefty $100,000 check each time a child's parents decide their child should undergo treatment—which, by the way, is rarely covered by health insurance.

In January 2023, President Trump unveiled his plan to protect Americans—specifically children—from these harmful practices.

- He will immediately sign an executive order to increase education on the subject and make it far easier for Americans who regret the gender transition medicine they received as children to sue their doctors.
- President Trump's executive order will also criminalize doctors who perform any form of gender transition medicine on children.
- President Trump will also allocate federal grants for doctors to research what *truly* causes gender dysphoria so our country can solve this problem at the root.

Our own Department of Justice considers female genital mutilation (FGM) in foreign nations—the process of cutting genitalia—a human rights abuse. It should be no different for Americans and especially our children.

CHAPTER 28

President Trump Will Save Women's Sports

Novelist Marc Levy writes, "If you want to know the value of one hour, ask the lovers waiting to meet . . . If you want to know the value of one minute, ask the person who just missed the bus. And if you want to know the value of one-hundredth of a second, ask the athlete who won a silver medal in the Olympics."

After the grueling hours of blood, sweat, and tears that are part of sports competitions, the very least that *any* athlete should be able to hope for is a fair playing field on game day. Instead, the Biden administration and the Democratic party have devised disgusting plans to further destroy scientific realities about gender and biology in true Orwellian fashion: by freely allowing men to compete against women in sports.

It is no secret that a simultaneous sleepy and woke Joe Biden and his Democrat puppet masters have waged war on women beginning on day one of his illegitimate regime. This war started with the Biden-Buttigieg massive supply-chain shortages that forced women to use mattress stuffing and cut-up dirty sheets as menstrual hygiene products.

This war on women and mothers continued with the malign neglect of key American baby formula factories experiencing malfunctions that killed children, left mothers unable to access adequate quantities of baby formula, and then blamed mothers for the problem on top of this.

Incredibly, the Biden regime also refused to investigate terrorist attacks on crisis pregnancy centers while simultaneously calling for them to be shut down. Yet, it gets worse.

During the fiftieth anniversary of the passage of Title IX of the Civil Rights Act of 1972, the Biden administration further proposed changing the definition of "sex" under Title IX—which the original ratifiers of the law understood to mean biological differences between males and females—to allow transgender athletes to compete on female sports teams. Biden's Department of Agriculture simultaneously took sweeping measures to strip meal funding for low-income children if their schools refused to comply with this ridiculous proposition.

Title IX under the Civil Rights Act ensured that all educational institutions in the United States rewarded male and female athletes equally. It has resulted in a more than 1,000 percent increase in female sports participation at the high school level and a 600 percent increase at the college level.

Athletic performance is undeniably impacted by biological make-up due to the fact that men have larger muscles, stronger bones, higher levels of testosterone, and higher rates of metabolizing and releasing energy. By allowing males to participate in these protected female athletic spaces, female athletes are unable to achieve the successes they would otherwise—and all of the various benefits (e.g., scholarships) that come with such success.

The world has already experienced the devastating impacts of this on the international scale: In February 2022, male swimmer Lia Thomas stole four swimming titles in the U.S. Division I women's Ivy League championships from several deserving women. In June 2021, male weightlifter Laurel Hubbard snatched Kuinini Manumua's last opportunity to compete at the Olympics away from her; and in May 2019, male track star CeCé Telfer breezed by eight of his opponents in the women's NCAA Division II national championship for 400-meter hurdles with nearly two seconds to spare at the finish line.

Here, it must be noted that college scholarships are of paramount importance to girls from low- and moderate-income families. They not only provide financial aid to offset the cost of tuition and other educational expenses, but they also unlock a world of new opportunities.

Through such opportunities, college education often leads to higher-paying jobs and greater economic stability, so scholarships can be a stepping stone to financial independence and social mobility. In doing so, they can break the cycle of poverty and uplift entire families. This is what is at stake for many female athletes now being pushed aside by transgender competitors.

There is also this affront: Women on sports teams with trans athletes—with male genitalia—are also faced with swallowing uncomfortable feelings about undressing and showering in the same locker rooms when there is already an extensive history of sexual assault in female athletics spaces.

To be clear, the Democrat transgender sports competition agenda is *deranged* and *dystopian*, and President Trump will put a stop to it when back in the White House. As soon as President Trump takes his oath of office, he should sign an executive order to protect women's athletics similarly to Representative Greg Steube's (R-FL) legislation, which passed the House in April 2023 with *zero* Democrat support.

President Trump's executive order should

- Ensure that Title IX language *only* recognizes an individual's reproductive biology and genetics at birth, as it was originally intended to.
- Remove *all* federal funding for schools that violate this law.
- Create the equal playing field female athletes have long fought for.
- Ensure female athletes will no longer have to fear giving up spots on teams, losing out on scholarships, and relinquishing their rightful positions on the victory podium to biological males.

CHAPTER 29

President Trump Will Make America Healthy Again

Big Pharma and Big Food have spent millions to keep Donald Trump out of the White House. They work hand in hand to make as much money as possible, and they are the cause of needlessly lethal mental and physical health problems for Americans for one simple reason: They care more about profits than American lives.

In his second term, Donald Trump will hold these deep-pocketed, deep-swamp creatures accountable for the massive harm they are inflicting upon the American population. Consider, here, that in the twenty-first century, 54 percent of American children are chronically ill while they face increased rates of anxiety, depression, autism, food allergies, obesity, developmental disorders, cancer, and more.

Yet, captured by special interests as they are, our federal agencies and politicians have paid little attention to these Dickensian conditions. Instead, they urge Americans to continue to over-vaccinate and consume unhealthy, often toxic, processed foods.

It's not for nothing that obesity is on a rocket ship rise in both American adults and children. Sadly, America now has one of the highest obesity rates in the world, and childhood obesity has tripled over the last three decades.

So, too, is autism an epidemic. Autism in American children has skyrocketed from 1 in 150 in the early 2000s to 1 in 36 today. In the 1990s, autism prevalence was just 1 in 1,000, and in the 1970s, 1 in 10,000. Just what is happening here?

Dr. Toby Rogers believes that the key to stopping the autism epidemic is ensuring toxins like mercury, ingredients in plastics and fire retardants, and certain ingredients in pharmaceuticals such as Tylenol, vaccines, and antidepressants are kept *out* of kids' bodies.

As for the obesity epidemic, Big Food delivers the average American child one hundred times more sugar than one hundred years prior, with sugar a substance as addictive as cocaine. This per capita sugar fix is a stark contrast to the 1950s, when the United States' obesity rate was virtually nonexistent.

Of course, Big Food hides this sugar in processed foods like Skittles and Campbell's soup, which also contains other harmful chemicals, including titanium dioxide, potassium bromate, bromi-nated vegetable oil, red dye no. 3, and propylparaben. These toxic chemicals disrupt estrogen, lower sperm count, cause cancer in animals and humans, disrupt healthy gut bacteria, damage our central nervous systems, cause memory loss and muscle coordina-tion loss, and are linked to hyperactivity in children.

Big Pharma is taking a similar toll. On the over-vaccination

front, the U.S. Centers for Disease Control and Prevention rec-
ommends children receive an astonishing *eleven* vaccinations in
their first *fifteen* months of life. That is nearly *double* the amount
of recommended vaccines for children in the 1990s and nearly
quadruple the amount of recommended vaccines for children
in the 1970s. And among these vaccinations is the experimental
COVID-19 quasi-vaccine, which has been linked to myocarditis,
nerve damage, and strokes.

Big Pharma regularly bribes doctors to coerce parents into
vaccinating their children. In 2016, Blue Cross and Blue Shield
reported that every pediatrician with an average of 260 children
under two years of age as patients was awarded $400 each time a
child completed ten vaccinations before their second birthday—a
potential $100,000 year-end bonus.

Additionally, Big Pharma whistleblower Calley Means dis-
cusses how Big Pharma and Big Food grossly target low-income
American children. She states that teenagers in low-income areas
are most likely to have pre-diabetes and obesity—which usually
means high cholesterol and blood sugar—from constantly eating
processed foods with toxic chemicals. Although these conditions
aren't lethal in and of themselves, they usually result in a lifetime
of dependence on medicines like statins, insulin, and Adderall,
keeping the money toward medical bills sky high.

Sadly, with obesity usually comes increased rates of depression.
Adults who struggle with obesity have a 55 percent increased risk
of developing depression over their lifetime compared to those
who do not. Currently, 30 percent of Americans admit to struggling with depression, which is a 10 percent increase from 2015.

To solve this, instead of examining Americans' living environment, the food they consume, the quality of water they drink, and more, Americans are being given Big Pharma prescriptions for antidepressant medications at a rate *triple* that of the previous decade. On top of this, these antidepressants have horrible side effects, including increased anxiety, insomnia, and even depression—the condition they are supposed to solve.

Without making serious changes to improve our national public health, our country will further grow unhealthy and weak.

President Trump is determined to make America healthy again. Our federal agencies must get back to the basics and figure out the root cause of the rapid increase of mental and physical disorders to properly solve them. President Trump should sign an executive order establishing a Presidential Commission on National Public Health. It would be led by the U.S. Food and Drug Administration and top scientists and nutritionists.

Their clear mission will be to lead an investigation into toxins given to Americans as young as several months old in both medicine and food, setting them up for a lifetime of illness. This commission will develop a list of toxic chemicals present in American processed foods to be immediately banned from all food production in the United States and publish a blueprint for solving crises that have been brought about in very large part by the irresponsible actions of Big Pharma and Big Food and their lobbyists.

CHAPTER 30

Breaking Up Big Tech
and Its Billionaire Oligarchs

by Mike Davis, Founder and President, Article III Project (A3P)

The monopolistic juggernauts of Big Tech, including the likes of Google, Facebook, Amazon, TikTok, and Apple, directed by the hands of self-styled "woke" billionaires—and for TikTok, by Communist China itself—exert an alarming degree of societal control over the American people. Their capacity to censor voices and manipulate the dissemination or concealment of news is starkly evident. As a topmost agenda in his second term, President Trump will dismantle these monopolies and reinstate the internet to the forces of market competition and the American citizenry.

President Trump will corral Big Tech through three key policy silos: privacy, antitrust, and "Section 230" reforms. Of these, the necessity for federal privacy legislation is arguably the most comprehensible and least disputed.

To begin, President Trump should vigorously back federal privacy legislation in Congress that empowers American consumers with authority over their data without imposing undue constraints on small businesses. An integral part of this strategy involves laying more stringent privacy requirements on large-scale platforms like Facebook that have systematically eroded American privacy rights for years.

In terms of antitrust, our current (and outdated) antitrust laws have routinely faltered in constraining what the pragmatic American perceives as online anticompetitive behavior. A classic example here is Apple's 30 percent "levy" imposed on small app developers via its app store or Amazon's pattern of decimating small businesses by strangling their access to Amazon's retail platform. Such practices will meet swift resistance in Trump's America.

In the previous Congress, reasonable legislation aimed at curtailing Big Tech's economic stronghold by modernizing our antitrust laws for the digital age garnered considerable bipartisan support in both the House and Senate, as well as from conservative tech advocacy groups like the Internet Accountability Project. Nevertheless, this bill hit a roadblock when Big Tech ally Senator Chuck Schumer (D-NY) denied it a floor vote.

In his second term, President Trump should firmly support this or similar legislation—and he won't hesitate to take on Democrats like Schumer who are deeply embedded with Big Tech, as well as libertarian Republicans in Congress and institutions like the Chamber of Commerce who are wary that such legislation could overly empower federal antitrust agencies.

These Chamber of Commerce libertarians represent a small segment of the conservative movement but wield substantial influence over tech policy. As a result, Congressional Republicans have sat on the sidelines while Big Tech has wreaked havoc on our nation, particularly on our children. This libertarian, laissez-faire approach to Big Tech has been a glaring failure for the American public. Even worse, it has eroded conservative values, which Congressional Republicans are duty-bound to uphold.

When it came to choosing between Big Tech and the national interest, President Trump made no bones about his position in his first term. This was evident when the Federal Trade Commission and the DOJ Antitrust Division filed suits against both Facebook and Google, respectively.

Reforming Section 230 is of paramount importance. Currently, Section 230 of the 1996 Communications Decency Act provides Big Tech platforms with legal immunity for content posted online. Under this protective cloak, leftist Big Tech tycoons have free rein to moderate—and censor—content at their discretion.

Section 230 also permits platforms like YouTube to host, promote, and profit from harmful content without bearing the societal costs of such content—with our children the biggest victims. This situation becomes particularly troublesome in the case of TikTok, controlled by Communist China, which enjoys Section 230 protection alongside U.S. Big Tech giants.

As if the promotion of harmful and malicious content weren't enough, Section 230 also enables Big Tech to censor lawful speech arbitrarily, including critical medical information during the COVID-19 pandemic. The Trump administration is dedicated to working with all groups to build a bipartisan coalition committed to breaking up Big Tech, a key mission of the Internet Accountability Project.

In alignment with his 2022 "Digital Bill of Rights," President Trump should

- Immediately issue an executive order prohibiting federal agencies from colluding with Big Tech to censor American citizens and from using taxpayer dollars to tag speech as misinformation by Big Tech platforms. The executive order will also halt taxpayer funding for any nonprofits and academic programs involved in online censorship.
- Release early Statements of Administration Policy (SAPs) expressing support for Big Tech antitrust legislation in Congress, federal privacy legislation, and Section 230 repeal or reform. These SAPs will act to keep a check on Big Tech allies within the executive branch who obstructed reform efforts during the first Trump administration.
- Through the FCC, revise the overly permissive, pro–Big Tech interpretations of Section 230 by lower courts. These interpretations have stretched the already troublesome statutory Big Tech immunities to absurd limits. The FCC has the statutory authority to carry out this task, being tasked with enforcing the 1996 Telecommunications Act (which houses Section 230).

Lastly, reflecting the axiom that personnel is policy, the second Trump administration will appoint experienced independent thinkers to chair the Federal Trade Commission, the Federal

Communications Commission, and the National Telecommunications and Information Administration (NTIA) at Commerce. Furthermore, President Trump will ensure that federal employees found to have actively engaged in censorship activities will face termination, and all national security officials will commit to a seven-year cooling-off period before accepting employment with a Big Tech platform.

CHAPTER 31

Stop E-Commerce from Inundating American Households with Counterfeits!

One of the most important tasks President Trump gave me in the Office of Trade and Manufacturing Policy during our years in the White House was to crack down on the sale of counterfeit and pirated products through e-commerce platforms like Amazon, eBay, and Alibaba. As President Trump noted in a landmark April 3, 2019, presidential memo:

> *Counterfeit trafficking impairs economic competitiveness by harming United States intellectual property rights holders and diminishing the reputations and trustworthiness of online markets; cheats consumers and poses risks to their health and safety; and may threaten national security and public safety through the introduction of counterfeit goods*

destined for the Department of Defense and other critical infrastructure supply chains.

Today, all the progress the Trump administration made is being thoroughly undermined by a Biden regime co-opted by the Amazon-eBay-Alibaba wing of the Big Tech lobby. Here's why shopping online in Joe Biden's America is like playing Russian roulette.

Buy something from Communist China online, and you have a one in ten chance or higher that the product is counterfeit. Such counterfeits will certainly cheat you. Some counterfeits— exploding batteries, faulty airbags, lead-laced toys—may even wind up killing you, a family member, or one of your beloved pets.

These short odds of getting ripped off online by Communist China are based on cold, hard data our office personally helped U.S. Customs and Border Protection (CBP) collect. In the White House, we worked with CBP to implement "Operation Mega-flex." This involved an enhanced search of parcels entering the United States at key ports of entry like Kennedy Airport and LAX.

Operation Mega-flex did indeed reveal an orgy of Communist Chinese counterfeit goods entering our country. In fact, two of the most heavily counterfeited—and dangerous—medications that arrive on American doorsteps courtesy of e-commerce are Lipitor and Viagra.

Many alleged Lipitor pills have no active ingredients whatsoever and are effectively heart attack pills. Many alleged Viagra pills have all too active ingredients like strychnine, which likewise can give you a heart attack.

Then, of course, there are the counterfeit electronic products that constitute the largest category of counterfeit commodities seized by CBP—more than 20 percent of all items seized each year. It's everything from phones, TVs, and kitchen appliances to extension cords and those power strips that can electrocute you or burn your house down.

And let's not forget the counterfeit automotive parts like brake pads, wheels, and seat belts that can have catastrophic consequences for drivers. Or the counterfeit bicycle helmets, another favorite of counterfeiters, that can lead to equally catastrophic consequences for cyclists.

The underlying problem is simply that counterfeiting, and its related cousin of piracy, represent highly profitable industries. For example, counterfeiters can keep production costs low by stealing product secrets or technological knowledge and exploiting new production technologies—for example, 3D printing has reduced the barriers to reverse engineering and the costs of manufacturing counterfeit products.

Lower production costs can also be achieved by manufacturing the counterfeit goods in a foreign market to lower the chances of detection and minimize legal liability. Such foreign-produced counterfeits can be combined with counterfeit labels, with the labels often applied to the products *after* the counterfeits arrive in the United States.

Of course, it is also much cheaper to manufacture illicit goods in countries like Communist China. Counterfeit and pirated goods are almost always produced in clandestine sweatshops.

Marketing costs are similarly lower. Setting up and maintaining an e-commerce website has far lower overhead than a brick-and-mortar retail outlet, while counterfeiters can also hijack images and descriptions of authentic products to confuse customers. In this online game, counterfeiters frequently open multiple seller accounts so that if one account is identified and removed, the counterfeiter can simply use another.

Social media has even gotten into the counterfeiting marketing act. The likes of Instagram and Facebook are alive with hashtags and connectivity algorithms that steer users unwittingly toward fake goods, particularly luxury brands.

When we were in the White House, the e-commerce platforms would squeal like stuck pigs when they were accused of facilitating counterfeiting. Amazon, in particular, and its lobbyists would shout from the mountaintop that the company had dramatically increased its expenditures on policing counterfeiting.

That claim was indeed true. However, the counterfeiting was increasing far faster than Amazon's spending on policing efforts, and one of the big reasons was Amazon was making so much money from the trafficking of counterfeit goods that it had little incentive to quash the counterfeit traffic.

Here, it must be noted that Amazon's business model is perversely conducive to the marketing of counterfeits. To wit: More than half of unit sales on Amazon are from independent merchants, and independents are far more likely to market counterfeits. And here's the perverse profit twist: These independent merchant transactions are typically far more profitable to Amazon than selling from its own warehouse because it takes a roughly 15 percent cut from the independents while avoiding inventory costs.

That third-party online marketplaces are riddled with counterfeits is reminiscent of Gresham's law, the economic axiom that "bad money drives out good." In this new digital Wild West, counterfeits from Communist China devalue legitimate brands from

American companies. The result is fewer American factories and jobs and a bigger trade deficit with Communist China.

In his second term in office, President Trump should rid e-commerce platforms like Amazon, Alibaba, and eBay of counterfeits. He will do so through dramatically increased search and seizure of foreign parcels purchased through e-commerce. Repeat offenders will be prohibited from selling products in the United States, and e-commerce platforms that are found to facilitate the importation of counterfeits through their business practices will face stiff fines and sanctions.

President Trump should also further empower agencies like the Federal Trade Commission and United States Trade Representative to crack down on counterfeiting and appoint personnel to these bureaucracies that will identify the elimination of counterfeiting as a key priority.

Most importantly, President Trump should use a combination of executive orders, regulatory change, and new legislation that will allow consumers the ability to seek both compensatory and punitive damages not just from the foreign producers, who are often impossible to find, but also from the e-commerce platforms themselves.

The abiding Trump principle here shall be clear: If e-commerce platforms profit from the sale of counterfeit and pirated goods—as they do to the tune of hundreds of billions of dollars annually—they must also bear the responsibility and costs of policing the market.

CHAPTER 32

Cracking Down on the "Wokefare" of American Corporations

The crucifixion of MyPillow CEO Mike Lindell by "wokefare" corporatists is the poster child of a new and dangerous form of uncivil warfare that threatens to further divide our nation even as it desecrates the First Amendment. As your forty-seventh president, Donald Trump will stop this wokefare in its tracks!

Similar to its close cousin "lawfare," wokefare seeks to bankrupt any business that does not conform to the rigid doctrines of the Left. Mike Lindell's original woke sin was to openly question the results of the 2020 presidential election.

Never mind there was abundant evidence of possible fraud and election irregularities in the 2020 race—particularly in the battlegrounds of Arizona, Georgia, Michigan, Nevada, Pennsylvania, and Wisconsin, where Biden allegedly won the race. (For details, read the Navarro Report penned in the White House after the reading of thousands of affidavits, the review of the lawfare tactics of Democrat strategists like Marc Elias, and the watching of enough video clips to send "JFK stole it from Nixon" chills up the spine.)

In pre-woke times, Mike Lindell would be praised across the ideological divide. He overcame a powerful drug and gambling addiction to create a powerhouse Made in the USA company employing thousands of Americans. In these wokefare times, however, Mike Lindell was put under constant attack.

Just how was wokefare waged against Mike Lindell? It started shortly after Joe Biden took office when America's Big Box and bedding retailers began choking off MyPillow's retail distribution channels.

From the Shopping Channel, Costco, and Dollar General to Kohl's, Target, and Walmart, more than twenty wokefare companies abruptly stopped selling MyPillow products. This, despite their popularity and profitability, and the hypocrisy of these woke corporatists is stunning.

To wit: In Woke Land, it's ethical to put a Made in the USA American company like MyPillow out of business if its CEO exercises his First Amendment rights. Yet, it's equally ethical for these woke retailers to stuff their distribution channels with Communist Chinese products made with slave labor in highly polluted factories that benefit from the massive theft of American intellectual property and equally massive, illegal government subsidies.

It didn't take long for the next wokefare jackboot to drop. It would come from Lindell's bank, the Minnesota Bank & Trust. Despite years of Mike's loyalty, this bank unilaterally closed all of his accounts, including the one for *Frank Speech*, Lindell's TV network and First Amendment megaphone.

Finally, in 2023, that paragon of wokefare virtue American Express went in for the wokefare kill. After a very profitable fifteen-year relationship with MyPillow, AmEx suddenly cut Lindell's credit line from a million dollars to a mere $100,000, thereby crippling Mike's ability to manage his cash flow. At the same time, Joe Biden's weaponized IRS was terrorizing MyPillow with multiple audits.

Mike Lindell is hardly a wokefare outlier. He is just the most public victim of an unrelenting wokefare now fragging patriots all over Trump's America.

President Trump will not tolerate such wokefare. By executive order, and through follow-up legislation he will sponsor, President Trump should reform our legal system in ways that will empower wokefare victims to hold both corporations *and* woke corporate executives *financially accountable* for their attacks and resultant damages. What goes around will indeed come around.

CHAPTER 33

President Trump Will Cancel "Cancel Culture" in Our K-12 Schools, Colleges, and Universities

One of the most corrosive threats to our freedom and very democracy is the meteoric rise of "cancel culture"—the spectacle of publicly shaming and punishing people or businesses for behavior outside the new and radical "woke" norms. As the National Association of Scholars (NAS) has noted in its groundbreaking research:

> *This new form of mob rule has dominated virtually every sector of American life for the last several years: politics, journalism, music & entertainment, sports, business, and of particular interest to the National Association of Scholars, higher education.*

During his first term, President Trump fought back hard against cancel culture. In a historic speech on July 4, 2020, at Mt. Rushmore, he noted on the 244th anniversary of the birth of our nation:

> *Our nation is witnessing a merciless campaign to wipe out our history, defame our heroes, erase our values, and indoctrinate our children. . . . One of their political weapons is "Cancel Culture"—driving people from their jobs, shaming dissenters, and demanding total submission from anyone who disagrees. This is the very definition of totalitarianism, and it is completely alien to our culture and our values, and it has absolutely no place in the United States of America.*

In that speech, President Trump had it exactly right when he noted both the scope of cancel culture and the myriad of ways this "Far Left fascism" and "Left-wing cultural revolution" is manifesting. Noted Trump:

> *In our schools, our newsrooms, even our corporate boardrooms, there is a new far-left fascism that demands absolute allegiance. If you do not speak its language, perform its rituals, recite its mantras, and follow its commandments, then you will be censored, banished, blacklisted, persecuted, and punished. It's not going to happen to us.*

Today, cancel culture continues its dangerous ascendancy under the regime of Joe Biden and a Democratic party infested with a radical and so-called "progressive" Left, and it is our schools and colleges and universities where America's children and young men and women are now most vulnerable both to its sting and its indoctrinating ways.

That cancel culture has infested our higher education system, in particular, is nothing short of a sacrilege. Historically, it is within the walls of our ivory tower campuses where professors, administrators, and students alike are supposed to be able to think and speak freely in their quest for truth and knowledge. Yet, in the ultimate perversion, far too many of our nation's campuses—virtually all heavily subsidized by American taxpayers and our government—have become fascist factories for the evolution of woke and radical dogma.

A key concept in understanding the perverse dynamics of cancel culture is that of the "Overton window," also known as the "window of discourse." The idea here is that there is an ever-evolving set of ideas and norms that define the range of policies that can be recommended in a society without appearing to be too extreme.

The problem now, however, is that within academia, for example, professors, students, and administrators cannot even express views within this moderate Overton window. As NAS has observed:

Academic administrators, students, and even professors risk "cancellation" when expressing viewpoints deemed unacceptable by the progressive ideologues ruling our colleges and universities. These allegedly abhorrent views need not be outside the Overton window—most aren't—to anger the progressive mob. Indeed, radical academics and bureaucrats have shifted the window steadily leftward, such that those who espouse ideas considered uncontroversial even a few years ago are anathematized.

The ever-growing catalog of case studies of cancel culture in academia compiled by NAS is as stunning as it is repugnant.

- Arizona State University fired an administrator simply for organizing an event featuring conservative speakers Dennis Prager and Charlie Kirk.
- Madera Community College in California put a gay, conservative professor on leave after he handed out chocolate made by a conservative company that featured the pronouns he/him and she/her on its bars.
- A liberal professor at Harvard was successfully pressured to resign as a member of the board of directors of a major oil company by Fossil Fuel Divest Harvard, an activist group at the university.
- Harvard also canceled a professor's talk on British Romanticism and philosophy, citing her board membership with the Woman's Liberation Front ("WoLF"), which they say is "an organization that takes a public stance regarding trans people as dangerous and deceptive."
- Down the road in Cambridge, an MIT professor had a prestigious public science lecture canceled because of an outrage mob on Twitter; she argued that diversity, equity, and inclusion (DEI) violated the ethical and legal principle of equal treatment and proposed an alternative framework called merit, fairness, and equality (MFE) whereby university applicants are evaluated based on their merit and qualifications alone.

- A Mayo Clinic College of Medicine and Science professor was suspended for commenting in newspapers about the positive benefits of plasma treatments for COVID-19 and for comments about the role of testosterone in boosting performance in trans athletes in women's sports.
- UCLA declined to provide a promised job offer after a group of more than fifty students complained about the professor's criticisms of "woke" ideology on his podcast.
- A Texas community college fired a biology teacher for alleged "religious preaching" after he taught a lesson about how sex is determined by X and Y chromosomes.
- Gonzaga University—a Jesuit Catholic institution—refused to allow a *pro-life* event by the campus Zags for Life group.
- A Western Kentucky University English instructor was protesting his school's political bias to embrace and enforce diversity, equity, and inclusion above free speech and academic freedom and discourse.
- COVID-19 dogma likewise extracted its pound of cancel-culture flesh. A Collin College professor was fired for challenging the school's COVID-19 response, while a student was forced to resign from Oklahoma State's student newspaper and a University of Southern Maine professor was fired after questioning mask mandates.

The list goes on and on—collated literally at the National Association of Scholars.

President Trump will decisively and promptly cancel "cancel culture" now metastasizing through our entire education system, from K–12 and colleges to our universities.

Our forty-seventh president will do so by using the power of executive orders and presidential memoranda to ensure that no educational institution that engages in cancel culture will receive federal funding of any kind from any government agency. No grants. No loans. No subsidies. No nothing. Period. Exclamation point!

CHAPTER 34

=================

Communist China's Cyber Attacks Must
Be Declared Acts of War

The Communist China landmass is roughly the same size as America. Yet, it has a population five times larger.

Noting Stalin's admonition that "quantity has a quality of its own," Communist China can overwhelm America militarily and economically if it is able to replicate our technologies and defense systems by stealing them. This is exactly what Communist China is quite successfully doing through its relentless and unrestricted cyber warfare.

Every day, drawing from its vast population, Communist China deploys vast cadres of cyber hackers to probe every conceivable institution of the American economy, society, and government.

The cyber game afoot with American *businesses* begins with the theft of intellectual property. Chinese state-owned enterprises can thereby beat American rivals with the added advantage of mercantilist tools like export subsidies and currency manipulation.

Yet, oftentimes, the goal of business hacking is to also gain a competitive advantage over an international rival through the acquisition of confidential internal documents. Such expropriated proprietary information allows a Chinese competitor to underbid or otherwise undermine a U.S. competitor.

When Communist China hacks our *personal* accounts, they are seeking to build profiles on us, particularly any of us who are critics of the Chinese Communist Party (CCP). Of course, criminal elements within the state-sponsored wing of China's hacking brigades are also busy stealing our money or identities, creating untold havoc in American lives.

Within *academia*, when Communist China hacks Harvard or MIT or the University of California, they are attempting to steal cutting-edge research—the *figurative* seed corn of our technical innovation. When Chinese bandits hack the computers of farm states' universities in Iowa or Kansas, they are *literally* trying to steal our seed corn.

Through its cyber hacks, Communist China has also acquired the blueprints of America's most sophisticated weapons systems—and thereby has significantly narrowed the technology gap between our militaries. For example, Communist China's fifth-generation jet fighters are very accurate knockoffs of America's most advanced planes, the F-22 and F-35. Here, with its manufacturing might, Communist China can build far more of these fifth-generation fighters than American taxpayers can afford—giving their military *both* Stalin-esque *quantity* and American *quality.*

Stealing our weapons systems is but one goal of Chinese hackers.

They seek to embed Trojan viruses throughout our military software. In a war scenario, they will drop our planes and satellites from the sky and misdirect the navigation systems of our missiles and ships.

It is long past time for the U.S. government to draw a very clear line in the sand with Communist China. They laugh at us now while Congress forms yet another committee to study its abuses but does nothing. They shake with mirth while Joe Biden and his Pentagon say we are in a "competition" rather than a "conflict" with China. They mock our FBI with its more than one thousand investigations of hacking going nowhere—even as that same FBI far more aggressively arrests and prosecutes so-called "domestic terrorists" guilty of nothing more than patriotism and standing up for their families and rights against a woke Left. Donald Trump should:

- Declare Communist Chinese cyber hacks as acts of war punishable by appropriately measured responses in kind.
- Direct the FBI and Department of Justice to treat China's cyber hackers not as criminals but as enemy combatants. While the J6 prisoners of war are stripped of their constitutional rights, China's hackers simply game our justice system and thereby clog up our courts. This will stop immediately under the new Trump administration.
- Order the release of all so-called "top secret" documents that will inform the American people of the real depth of the Chinese hacker threats.

Donald Trump is the only U.S. president in modern history to stand up to Communist China. He will do so again, particularly in this dangerous cyber warfare arena.

CHAPTER 35

Protecting Taiwan's Strategic Value to the United States

by James Fanell and Bradley A. Thayer

The Chinese Communist Party (CCP) is determined to conquer Taiwan and the United States must deter this outcome for our own national survival. While the CCP's intent has been constant since 1949, Xi Jinping now has the capability to execute a military invasion of the island.

Taiwan is strategic to the United States' national security for four reasons. The first is economic. Taiwan is a vibrant and wealthy economy—and a superpower in computer chip production. Any damage to its factories, including their destruction—or conquest—by China will reverberate for many years throughout the U.S. and global economies.

Second, Taiwan occupies a key geostrategic position both

Beijing and Washington recognize. For China, Taiwan is the cork in the bottle of the first island chain, and so prevents the People's Liberation Army Navy (PLAN) and Air Force (PLAAF) from easily accessing the entirety of the Pacific Ocean. Physical control of Taiwan further expands the PRC's power into the Sea Lines of Communication (SLOC) of the western Pacific and directly threatens the U.S.—and allied—military operations.

Third, in the realm of political warfare, Taiwan is a strong democracy that represents what the PRC might have been had the CCP not come to power. Taiwan's very existence is a daily reminder of this reality and why the CCP is an illegitimate regime.

Fourth, Taiwan is a symbol of U.S. credibility to resist Chinese aggression and thus sustain its viability. Standing with Taiwan provides a tangible indication the United States will resist the PRC's expansionism and will do so with substantial investment from U.S. and allied forces.

Before the PRC attacks, Americans must understand how U.S. interests would be affected if Taiwan were to fall. U.S. national security would be greatly harmed for reasons that include:

First, the acquisition of Taiwan's dynamic population of almost twenty-four million, and its $800 billion economy, would be a great fillip to the PRC's perceived comprehensive national power and a relative, and significant, loss for the United States.

Second, the loss of Taiwan's chip production would be a major, perhaps even mortal, blow to many U.S. firms and a colossal shock to the U.S. economy. The next largest chip maker, South Korea's Samsung, as well as other firms like Intel, would not be able to address the shortfall.

After the fall of Taiwan, South Korea would be surrounded and under great pressure from the PRC, North Korea, and Russia. In the worst, and most likely case, this pressure would push Seoul to abandon its alliance with the United States and drift into the PRC's orbit.

Third, other U.S. allies, including Japan and the Philippines, would fall under the shadow of an emboldened PRC. Japan would confront difficult choices, including immediate danger to the Senkaku Islands.

While Tokyo might resist the PRC, including through nuclear proliferation, it also might not keep its alliance with the United States. If Tokyo sees the United States fail to defend Taiwan, what assurances would it have that the U.S. would assist Japan in the event of PRC aggression?

For the Philippines, everything would depend upon the United States' willingness to provide a credible extended deterrent, given the PRC's expansion would not stop at Taiwan. Having been betrayed by the Obama administration in 2012 at Scarborough Shoal, and under tremendous pressure today at Second Thomas Shoal, the Philippines is already on the front lines of the PRC's expansion.

Fourth, two of America's treaty allies would also be impacted by the PRC's successful invasion of Taiwan, Australia, and the Kingdom of Thailand. While the Australians have been steadfast partners in the fight against the PRC, the fall of Taiwan would essentially allow the PRC to extend a "bar of steel"—the PLA—from the eastern shores of Taiwan to the PRC's recent positions of influence in the Solomon Islands and out to Kiribati. This PRC-controlled sea line of communication would effectively cut Australia and New Zealand from the United States. Likewise, the

Kingdom of Thailand would be under even more pressure to go along with Beijing's strategic design for Southeast Asia.

Finally, a CCP-occupied Taiwan would allow the PRC's military to have a new military base from which it has direct access to the Pacific for China's navy and air force to project power against U.S. forces in South Korea, Japan, Australia, the Philippines, Malaysia, Singapore, and Indonesia, as well as those in Guam, Hawaii, Alaska, and the U.S. homeland.

Given these strategic considerations, it is critical that a new Trump administration help Taiwan develop a robust conventional deterrent augmented by a stronger U.S. presence. This requires the following:

- Support, training, and armament are needed to defend the missions related to sea denial and coastal defense. This requires weapons systems: thousands of sea mines, hundreds of harpoons and SM-6 supersonic anti-ship cruise missiles, the transfer of more minelayers and minesweepers from allied fleets, and more SSKs from Japan and Korea to Taiwan.
- Support, training, and armament needed for integrated air and missile defense. As in South Korea, Terminal High Altitude Area Defense systems should be deployed to Taiwan.
- Ability for Taiwan to strike land-based targets in the PRC by air- and land-based Taiwanese assets.
- Prepositioned supply for sustained operations. The ability to rapidly resupply Taiwan by air and sea with dedicated prepositioned material unit sets in Taiwan (two U.S. divisions), Okinawa, and the Philippines.
- Exercises on Taiwan testing Taiwanese and United States

Indo-Pacific Command (USINDOPACOM) air operations on civilian roads and exercises on runway and tarmac repair.

- Stress testing INDOPACOM for defeating blockade and air and naval resupply of Taiwan under fire.

CHAPTER 36

The Trump "America First" Doctrine of Foreign Policy Must Be Restored in 2025

by Ric Grenell, former acting director of National Intelligence and Ambassador to Germany during the Trump administration.
This chapter is based on Ric's speech at the Nixon Library.

Prior to the coming of President Donald Trump in 2017, American foreign policy was driven by a Washington establishment that cared little for America's national interest. Instead, our foreign policy establishment spent decades through presidencies, from the Bushes and Clinton through Obama-Biden, implementing foreign policy on the basis of strategically bankrupt moral and political maxims.

Through such "missionary diplomacy," America's foreign policy establishment counted on illusive and illusory "transitions to democracy" in countries like Communist China and Iran to pacify dangerous strategic rivals. We as a nation conducted humanitarian interventions without regard for the inevitable humanitarian fallout. We signed resolutions and protocols we never had the ability to implement. Most egregiously, we committed ourselves to wars in Afghanistan and Iraq without a clear understanding of the threats we faced or the outcomes we could realistically achieve.

It was my experience as U.S. spokesman to the UN during the first five years of the Iraq War that eventually convinced me that a costly military engagement without a clear benefit to the American people carries profound social and political risks—and drew me to Donald Trump's presidency.

By 2016, the American people had indeed grown tired of being told that the national interest was an immoral consideration. For four beautiful years after his election, President Trump restored American nationalism in the White House and conducted American foreign policy under the flag and banner of a "Trump Doctrine" that married strategy and moral clarity in a way that had eluded both Richard Nixon and Ronald Reagan and had been foreign to the likes of Bill Clinton, George W. Bush, and the globalist duo of Barack Obama and Joe Biden.

The Trump Doctrine puts the security and prosperity of the American people before everything else. While there are other important goals of our foreign policy—such as human rights and democratization—none would be pursued in the Trump White House at the expense of our national defense and economic well-being.

This Trump Doctrine is not just a *sound* basis for foreign policy. It is also a *moral* foreign policy for at least three good reasons.

First, the Trump Doctrine is a pure expression of representative government. It places, above all else, the interests of the sovereign and self-determining American people. Under the Trump Doctrine, the President of the United States works for the American people and unapologetically pursues the U.S. national interest without pretext or apology.

Second, the Trump Doctrine forces policy makers to be clear-eyed—to see the world as it is, not as they think it ought to be. While moving the world toward greater freedom and liberty is, and always will be, an important goal for the American people, the Trump Doctrine forces policy makers to align our objectives with our capabilities—to match our goals with what is truly attainable in the world in which we live.

In contrast, when our rhetoric surpasses our resources, when our policy exceeds our capabilities, when our expectations cloud our judgment, and when our desire to remake the world overtakes our duty to the American voter—that is when you get point-less and costly wars. That is when you send America's sons and daughters into harm's way without a plan for what comes next. That is when you make disastrous trade deals and sign dangerous nuclear agreements. That is when you get massive inequality, and a divided society. That is when you get an *immoral* foreign policy.

Third, a foreign policy based on the national interest, reasonably defined, is more durable, and more predictable, than one based on the passions and furies of the moment. Here, "America First" does not mean "America alone."

By openly pursuing our interests, the United States can build consensus among other countries whose own interests reflect similar ideals and objectives. Indeed, America's alliances are one of our greatest advantages in an era of renewed strategic competition with Communist China, Iran, and a revanchist Russia.

Because the United States and Europe share the values of security, peace, and free trade, President Trump asked, nay *demanded,* during his first term that our European allies share the burden of transatlantic security. President Trump wanted Europe to become a political and military power because he was—and remains—confident that our shared values will provide the fuel for that power.

As the largest economy and de facto leader of Europe, Germany will ultimately decide the strength of NATO, and thus of European security. It is for the sake of Europe's security that President Trump sought to hold our German partners to their NATO obligations.

Likewise, when President Trump reviewed America's security arrangement with Japan or our trade relationship with India in his first term, it was not because he questioned the value of our partnership with those two great allies. On the contrary, it was because he wanted to encourage our Indo-Pacific partners to become more confident and to play a more active global role in defending our shared values.

Whether they admit it or not, those in the globalist establishment who criticize this nationalist approach advocate for keeping our allies subdued and passive. However, President Trump does not believe that American or global security will benefit from keeping nations that share our interests in a position of perpetual dependency. It is only by having nimble and outward-looking allies that the United States can continue to play the role of global superpower effectively!

For those countries that do *not* share our values and goals, President Trump is not waiting around for the arc of history. The Trump Doctrine seeks to incentivize our adversaries to change their behavior, not mobilize forces to replace them.

He does not make regime change a precondition for negotiations. Instead, the president is determined to outcompete our adversaries and willing to cut deals where American and global security will benefit.

During President Trump's first term, you watched how the Trump Doctrine played out in real time with Communist China, Iran, Russia, and North Korea. You were far safer under the Trump Doctrine than you are today under Biden. Today, all four of these dangerous strategic rivals are far bolder in challenging the United States under weak Joe Biden leadership.

After almost four years of Joe Biden, you know this now in your bones: The national interest, or as President Trump says it best, "America First," is simply the best means of ensuring the security and prosperity of the American people, cooperating with those who share our values, and outcompeting our adversaries.

America First is also the best way to retain the support of the American public, without which no foreign policy can survive. And America First is the only way public support can be legitimately called upon, when—as does happen in the course of our history—we are locked in a confrontation in which we must use all of our power and strength to win.

The Trump administration's ability to defeat ISIS without a large use of boots on the ground, without triggering a conflict with Russia, and without causing a new wave of terror offers a shining example that an America First strategy works. And

Trump's triumph over ISIS with minimal U.S. engagement salvaged the public support that our predecessors lost in Libya, Syria, and Iraq.

Of course, America First critics will call it everything from "nativist" to "isolationist" to "fascist." Perhaps our best rejoinder is to begin with what the Trump Doctrine is *not*.

It is not based on any race or color or creed. It does not advance the interests of one group of Americans at the expense of any other. It has no bias with regard to red versus blue, or urban versus rural. It is not a doctrine based on class or status, nor does it aim to please the members of a professional elite or the Washington establishment.

Rather, the Trump Doctrine is the belief that our government must focus on the equality and dignity of every American—from Maine to Hawaii, Texas to Minnesota, Oregon to Puerto Rico— and that this obligation is fulfilled by promoting the security and prosperity of the American people, not by pretending to promote the interests of all humanity.

To me, this is "America First." This is the Trump Doctrine. This is American exceptionalism for the twenty-first century.

As ground-breaking as it is in our time, President Trump has drawn on a great tradition in American foreign policy.

Think of George Washington's warning against foreign entanglements, cautioning us not "to implicate ourselves, by artificial ties," in the storms of foreign upheavals.

Think of Teddy Roosevelt's caution that "it would be both foolish and an evil thing for a great and free nation to deprive itself of the power to protect its own rights."

Or think of John Quincy Adams, who said that America "goes

not abroad in search of monsters to destroy," but "is the well-wisher to the freedom and independence of all."

We would have done well to heed these words in years past. Joe Biden has completely forgotten them as he bumbles us into an ever more dangerous future.

Donald Trump will bring these words right back into the White House in 2025, and both America and the world will quickly become safer and more prosperous places.

CHAPTER 37

America Shall Not Sleep by the Light of a Communist Chinese Moon

by Greg Autry, director for Space Leadership, Policy, and Business,
Thunderbird School of Global Management at Arizona State University

The space policies of President Donald J. Trump's first administration were the most significant and successful since JFK committed our nation to beating the Soviets to the Moon. While later presidents squandered America's lead with a series of failed exploration initiatives, President Trump's program succeeded and still moves forward.

After Trump reestablished the National Space Council and created the United States Space Force, his bold vision captured both broad bipartisan support in Congress and that of the Biden White House. Project Artemis has returned NASA spacecraft to the Moon; a second Trump administration will move America's space program forward at warp speed.

NASA is the unquestioned global leader in space and no nation can challenge the capabilities of our Space Force. Yet, Communist China is moving aggressively into the high frontier, with plans to explore, occupy, and undoubtedly claim critical portions of the Moon.

While the Trump team originally targeted "boots on the Moon" for 2024, that date is now slipping toward 2027. Meanwhile, Communist China has announced a 2030 Moon landing, and it has been relentlessly on time in its space efforts.

Beating the world's most populous prison nation to the Moon would, of course, once again demonstrate the superiority of American technology and grit. Yet far more importantly, the Moon is a nearby and unoccupied "continent" the size of Africa. It is filled with a cornucopia of untapped resources of untold value to the American people and businesses here on Earth. It also represents an essential giant step for humankind's eventual settlement of the solar system.

A second Trump administration will ensure that everyone benefits from this new frontier. Under American leadership and an American flag, it will be American values, rather than Communist China's "Xi Jinping Thought," that are carried into the solar system with the next human diaspora.

Winning the second space race won't be accomplished entirely with large governmental programs, like the Chinese leviathan is relying upon. Instead, capitalist America must leverage the power of America's world-class aerospace giants and the genius of our disruptive space entrepreneurs.

Trump's Space Policy Directive 2 called for streamlining regulations to "minimize uncertainty for taxpayers, investors, and private industry." Much of that task remains incomplete and must be reinvigorated.

A second Trump White House will also reorganize the U.S. government to accelerate America's natural commercial advantage.

On his first day in office, POTUS47 should sign an executive order restoring the Office of Space Commerce and the Office of Commercial Space Transportation to their Reagan-era positions, reporting directly to the secretaries of those departments.

Space is now a half-trillion-dollar industry and growing faster than most other industrial sectors. It demands top-level attention and cover.

Keeping a space environment increasingly crowded with satellites accessible is critical. The United States will continue to lead by completing the transfer of space situational awareness data and space traffic management responsibilities solely to the Office of Space Commerce.

Here, there must be a clear division of labor: The FCC must be entirely focused on its job of allocating and protecting the radio spectrum. The Office of Commercial Space Transportation will be instructed to further streamline and accelerate the review process for spaceports and launch systems.

Within the Pentagon, the turf battles must end. The U.S. Space Force, founded under Trump, has remained constrained by its subservient position within the USAF. Meanwhile, the fighter jocks who run the Air Force see space as only a tool for augmenting U.S. warfighting capabilities in the air and on the ground. While the Air Force does that job admirably, it is time for the Space Force to leave the nest and assume a future-forward role of protecting

U.S. governmental and commercial interests in an increasingly congested and conflicted cis-lunar space.

Developing the nearly infinite resources of our solar system requires that U.S. firms are able to compete under free market rules. The outdated and outmoded 1967 Outer Space Treaty precludes national sovereignty and does not allow for real property rights on celestial bodies. Establishing ownership of real estate for lunar mines, space factories, and hotels is critical if American developers are to collateralize, and eventually sell, the value they have created with their capital and hard work. We cannot build a future based entirely on government grants and venture capital; we must engage all of America's world-class financial sector. U.S. commercial operators encroached by domestic competitors or foreign governments must have a clear path to adjudication and enforcement. In the absence of sovereignty, there can be no rule of law.

Leaving our commerce to the mercies of a sluggish, corrupt UN process dominated by Communist China and its proxies is worse than no solution. Unpoliced frontiers have a notorious history of conflict and human rights abuses.

Clarifying the rule of law for commercial and governmental actors on celestial bodies is essential to ensuring peace in space. If we do not renegotiate this agreement, we can be sure that Chinese state-owned banks will fund China's operators and Communist China will effectively claim lunar territory, regardless of any treaty they have signed. Americans will, and must, not sleep by the light of a Chinese Communist Moon during a second Trump administration.

Epilogue

While Trump promised nothing on criminal justice
reform but still did something significant, Biden
promised a lot but so far has done nothing of real
substance. For those of us who don't want Trump
to be re-elected, this is an uncomfortable truth.

— Mark Oster, Clemency Expert, CNN

To paraphrase the great Mark Twain, the coldest winter I ever spent was a spring in a Miami prison. I entered Federal Correctional Institution Miami courtesy of a Democrat railroading on March 19, 2024, shortly after handing off the balance of this manuscript to Donald Trump Jr. and Sergio Gor. That first night in the slammer was the closest I would come to dying in prison—at least thus far about one month into a four-month stretch.

It was almost comical. I spent that entire first night on a bunk bed mattress barely as wide as my frame under a blanket the thickness of tissue paper shivering my rear end off.

The air outside my 45-man dorm was a tropical 80 degrees, but it was in the 50s inside my dorm because the air conditioner was on full blast and the thermostat didn't work; it hadn't worked for over a year. So the prison was spending an extra $2,000 a month on electricity bills for want of a $75 repair. That was a metaphor for the whole place—a massive waste of taxpayer funds.

That's the very first thing that struck me in my first weeks—the money and precious time wasted warehousing men serving sentences in many cases *far* too long for the crimes they committed.

Don't get me wrong. I haven't gone soft on crime just because I wound up behind bars (I hasten here to add for simply doing my duty to the Constitution, my oath of office, and my commander in chief).

But during my prison experience, I've learned firsthand that we need to be just as smart on crime as we are tough. I found myself among over 150 souls, most of whom were first-time and nonviolent offenders. Many were serving mind-numbingly long sentences far in excess of the time necessary for a "just" punishment, sentences which would not only destroy these men but would also damage their families and any future they might have together.

Consider Inmate One, for example. He'd been in for over 20 years. At the tender age of 66 and in a wheelchair struggling with deteriorating health, he had been repeatedly denied compassionate release. Or Inmate Two. Another wheelchair-bound, 20-plus-year white-collar prisoner who had entered on his own two legs in his 50s. Why in the name of God was he still behind bars?

And then there were two other guys down the bunk line suffering with severe prostate and lung cancer. At least the prison was providing some chemotherapy, but again, why were they still here?

But it was the young men growing into middle age in prison

who in some sense represented the biggest tragedy of oversentencing. They were there for some kind of wire fraud or overbilling of Medicare or the private health insurers or for inflating some numbers to get a bigger government loan or for the garden-variety dope deal.

In each case, the government would coerce them into a plea deal, strip them of their assets (often leaving their wives and children to live at the poverty line on government aid), and keep them in prison long enough for their skills to deteriorate—making them difficult to employ when they finally got out in a hundred or two hundred months.

And that's the stupidity of it all. While we should damn well harshly punish criminals for the crimes they commit, the goal should not be to break them, but simply to inflict punishment enough that they *never* break the law again. And here's the basic economics:

For every day a prisoner stays in prison past the time necessary to deter future crimes, there's a fundamental waste of taxpayer funds—*and* a lost opportunity for that freed prisoner to become a worker or entrepreneur that will contribute to the tax base. Think about it this way:

An inmate who stays too long in prison wastes taxpayer money—about $50,000 a year. This inmate is not out participating in the American economy and therefore is not paying taxes as a productive citizen. That's the fiscal double whammy of oversentencing.

And of course that prisoner is also taking up precious prison space and resources that could be used to incarcerate violent and repeat offenders—the most dangerous career criminals who belong behind bars and off our streets.

This is a very roundabout way of saying that prisons right now are "Trump Country" for one very important reason: President Trump's signing of the 2018 First Step Act (FSA).

The FSA is a piece of legislation that provides nonviolent and first-time offenders—no murderers, rapists, or child molesters allowed—with an accelerated timetable for release. For every 30 days an inmate serves as a good citizen, he or she would get 10 days off from their sentence, and this time can accumulate.

Inmates love Donald Trump for providing this opportunity, just as many hate Joe Biden's administration for refusing to fully implement the FSA. They also hate Joe Biden even more than they love Trump because it was Senator Biden who spearheaded the barbaric "mandatory minimum" sentences that have led to the massive oversentencing of first-time offenders.

But the FSA and Biden's sadistic mandatory minimums are not the only reasons Donald Trump has strong support within the walls that now hold me in—and my lovely fiancée and family out. Most folks here are just that—plain folks and Deplorables whose families are struggling on the outside to make ends meet as inflation ravages their budgets. Meanwhile a horde of illiterate illegal aliens floods across our borders into our labor markets, thereby driving down the wages of, and stealing jobs from, Black, brown, and blue-collar Americans—who are heavily represented in prison.

That's one of the many things the woke Bidenites don't understand. Black, brown, and blue-collar Americans collectively have more wisdom than any gaggle of radical Democrats up on Capitol Hill who are now driving the American bus right over a fiscal cliff.

These are the people with whom I am doing my time. The most

pleasant surprise I have found among the inmates has been the support that so many offer one another.

So while Hunter Biden and the Biden crime family remain free despite Hunter's unspeakable acts and their selling America off to the Communist Chinese, I will do my time at FCI Miami courtesy of a kangaroo J6 committee, a Democrat Congress, a Democrat-run Department of Justice, an Obama-appointed district judge, a Washington, D.C., Democrat jury, and three Democrat-appointed appeals court judges now running a weaponized system of injustice—and take comfort and gather strength from the thousands of letters of support I have received from Trump's America.

While the Biden regime takes my freedom (and plots to put Donald Trump himself in prison) this important New MAGA Deal book will go to the printers and be ready for release on my birthday, July 15, 2024—the same week I will be free of this god-forsaken place and hopefully be on a plane with my beloved Pixie to fly to Milwaukee to see and hear Donald John Trump accept the Republican nomination for president.

In the meantime, I will eat bad food stuffed with sugar and carbs and devoid of protein and fresh anything, be counted five times a day at my bunk, sleep in an icebox with 45 other men and share five toilets and showers with them, have limited access to my family, and live largely cut off from the world of news and the information I need to prepare the appeal of my case.

Your mission (should you choose to accept it), as I remain behind bars, is to get out and do *everything* you can to ensure Donald Trump is our next and 47th president.

I've tried in this book to give you all the tools and information you need to explain to skeptics why MAGA policies are the most sensible in the world and how Donald Trump is going to pull this nation back from the Biden brink of economic chaos, fiscal profligacy, an overrun border, woke school and transgender propaganda, and the very real existential threats posed by the likes of Communist China, Iran, North Korea, Russia, growing cadres of drug and human trafficking cartels, and a beyond-dangerous diaspora of radical Islamic terrorists.

The New MAGA Deal promise of this book consists of 100 (and more) immediate Trump actions to take back Trump's America from the radical and woke anti-patriots who have seized power. This book can show you the way—share it with a friend!

I hope to see you on the other side.

Concluding Thoughts

After reading this book, you know what Donald John Trump will likely do as our forty-seventh president. And you know his policies offer the best path to peace, prosperity, and national security built on a solid MAGA foundation of a strong manufacturing base, secure borders, and an end to endless wars—all in the name of God, country, and family.

As the Oakland Raiders' owner Al Davis used to say: "Just win, baby!" Help Trump win by spreading the gospel of MAGA and getting out to vote!

And *please* share this guidebook with a friend.

Author's Note: Valentine's Day, 2024

As I write this note, I am getting ready to go to a federal prison to be punished for an alleged crime that no senior White House official has *ever* been charged with in the history of our Republic.

Here's what is so incongruous about this turn of the Democrat screw: The Department of Justice itself (DOJ), for more than fifty years, has maintained a policy that senior White House advisers and "alter egos of the president," as we are called, absolutely cannot be compelled to testify before Congress.

The DOJ has maintained this policy across Democrat and Republican administrations to protect the constitutional separation of powers in the critical role that a president's use of executive privilege plays in ensuring the type of confidentiality a president needs in order to make his best decisions. Yet, prosecuted and convicted I was by a DOJ in direct contradiction to a more than fifty-year-old policy.

Of course, my case is on appeal—likely to the Supreme Court. Here, I have said from the outset, after receiving a congressional subpoena from a kangaroo court otherwise known as the J6 Committee, that my case would certainly go the legal distance.

After all, mine is a landmark case in constitutional law, a clear case of "first impressions." It is a case that has the potential of forever defining the scale and scope of the constitutional separation of powers as it implicates executive privilege and partisan attempts by the legislative branch to destroy that separation.

If I win, the constitutional separation of powers will be preserved, and America wins. If I lose, going forward in time, partisan Congresses will forever shower the White House with subpoenas, harass political opponents, and hamstring the executive branch.

Given these high stakes, here's another remarkable aspect of my case. The judge in my case—truth be told, a Democrat political operative in a black robe—refused to allow me to remain free pending my appeal. This is indeed remarkable because my case involves numerous substantial issues that may lead to either a reversal or a retrial—this is beyond dispute. Yet this judge, who is an Obama-Biden appointed judge and up to his neck in political influence, refused to do the right thing and what any other judge with any kind of objectivity would have done.

But don't cry for me Argentina. That's not why I'm raising this issue in this conclusionary author's note.

I'm simply pointing my own situation out because as bad as it is, Donald Trump's situation is far worse—we may both wind up in prison. Indeed, Trump is being pursued on at least four different judicial fronts by Democrat jackals, two in federal court, one in Georgia, and one in New York.

Like my case, what all of these Trump cases share in common is their partisan nature.

In my case, I was held in contempt by a Democrat-controlled Congress. I was prosecuted by a Democrat-controlled Department of Justice. I was arrested by armed FBI dragoons and put in leg irons at the direction of a Democrat DOJ lawyer with a clear anti-Trump bias. I was stripped of all possible defenses before my case went to a jury by a Democrat judge who, along with his wife, raised tens of thousands of dollars for Barack Obama and then was appointed by Obama as a judge. And I was given the harshest possible sentence and denied release pending appeal as I normally would have been in the absence of partisan considerations.

In Trump's case, he, too, was the target of an armed FBI raid—in his case at Mar-a-Lago. Every single prosecutor in his criminal cases is a Democrat. At the federal level, all those who are trying to put him in prison, or at least keep him off the 2024 ballot and out of the White House, are Democrats operating at the direction and pleasure of Trump's political rival Joe Biden.

And did I mention, it is a Democrat judge in New York that is stripping him of his wealth in a bogus prosecution no one has ever been subject to.

It is no wonder that the American people no longer have any confidence in our FBI or our justice system. When more than half of the American people think that our justice system has become weaponized for partisan purposes, that can do nothing but undermine the very fabric of our society and political institutions.

It's no wonder that Donald Trump goes up in the polls every

time another Democrat partisan raises his or her ugly head with yet another indictment or subpoena.

The BIG POINT I want to make here, as it very much pertains to this book, is that this 2024 presidential election will of course be about a wide range of critical policy issues. It is precisely the mission of this book to inform every American voter about how Donald Trump is likely to tackle these key issues in a second term in the White House as our forty-seventh president.

As you have read, this book covered the key issues, from the economy and border security to foreign policy and a wide range of social issues related to everything from transgender intrusions into women's sports to putting an immediate halt to the mutilated initiation of our children's genitals under the false flag of gender identity.

Yet, it is also undeniable—and nobody knows this better than I, given the quite literal trial I'm being put through—that the 2024 election will also be a referendum.

It will be a referendum on whether it is appropriate for partisans seizing power to weaponize our judicial system.

Even more important, it will be a referendum on whether Donald Trump should be put in prison—or, at a minimum, the American people should be denied a chance for Trump to serve as our next president.

My fervent hope is that the broad swath of American voters will just as warmly embrace the Trump 2024 agenda analyzed in this book as they reject the weaponization of our judicial system and what are long-standing abuses by the Federal Bureau of Investigation.

I want to be crystal clear here. Neither I nor Donald Trump

seek retribution against our political enemies. Yet, it is critically important that all of those who have engaged in the political persecution of Donald Trump and a large cadre of his political, legal, and policy advisers be held *accountable* for their actions.

I note here for the record that virtually every single senior adviser I served with in the White House who continued to support or work with Donald Trump after the 2020 election has been the target of unrelenting lawfare, which is nothing more nor less than the perversion of our judicial system to advance partisan ends.

Each of these advisers I served with—names like Mark Meadows, Dan Scavino, John Eastman, Jeff Clark, Mike Flynn, Rudy Giuliani, Jenna Ellis, and Stephen Miller—all have been subpoenaed and/or indicted and have had to endure legal costs that collectively have stretched into the tens of millions. America's greatest mayor Rudy Giuliani himself is on the brink of bankruptcy, while my legal fees are well in excess of a million dollars. Men like Eastman and Clark face an unfair disbarment by, no surprise here, Democrat-controlled bar associations.

This is an abomination, and in addition to promptly tackling all of the big policy issues covered in this book, a second Trump administration must and will put an end to the weaponization of the judicial system, eliminate what has become a dual system of injustice under Biden rule, and thereby restore confidence in our judiciary.

My own view is that the FBI must be broken down to the very ground and replaced with a new organization that forever sheds a toxic organizational culture of political intimidation that goes back to the days of J. Edgar Hoover and his spying on political targets like Martin Luther King Jr., JFK, and Robert F. Kennedy

Jr., plus a gaggle of congressmen Hoover would "get the goods on" and then blackmail so he could stay in power.

Today's FBI is no better than Hoover's. I have had their guns pointed at me firsthand and felt their handcuffs and leg irons for doing nothing more than my duty to the country, the Constitution, and my president. I've looked these agents in the eye and I've seen them on the news harassing Donald Trump at gunpoint.

My own view, too, is that every single FBI agent and attorney involved in the prosecution and persecution of Donald Trump needs to be investigated both by Congress and the Department of Justice itself. If any of these people are found to have colluded with each other in the White House or Congress or political operatives outside the government, or to have knowingly engaged in election interference, they should be held accountable for what is, stripped of rhetoric, nothing more than an attempted coup.

I hope, then, you find this book as enjoyable and informative to read as I found it as enjoyable and important to write. And I am honored to have such a distinguished group of co-authors and former Trump officials who served so honorably in the Trump White House—and may do so again.

To paraphrase the most famous quote of the now deceased Oakland Raiders football team owner, Al Davis: Just Vote! Just Vote for Donald Trump on November 5, 2024, and all our lives will get better.

At no time in American history has a presidential election been more important.

Appendix A: The Navarro Report Summarized

Author's Note: For almost four years, I have had to endure classic media spin about how the 2020 presidential election was somehow a fair one. Nothing I have seen since I authored the Navarro Report in January 2021 has dissuaded me from a very informed belief that the fix for Joe Biden was in. Read this summary and you'll get the big picture. The full report is on my website at www.peternavarro.com

At the stroke of midnight on Election Day 2020, President Donald J. Trump appeared well on his way to winning a second term. He was already a lock to win both Florida and Ohio; no Republican has ever won a presidential election without winning Ohio, while only two Democrats have won the presidency without winning Florida.

At the same time, the Trump-Pence ticket had substantial and seemingly insurmountable leads in Georgia, Pennsylvania, Michigan, and Wisconsin. If these leads held, these four key battleground states would propel President Trump to a decisive 294 to 244 victory in the Electoral College.

Shortly after midnight, however, as a flood of mail-in and absentee ballots began entering the count, the Trump red tide of victory began turning Joe Biden blue. As these mail-in and absentee ballots were tabulated, the president's large leads in Georgia, Pennsylvania, Michigan, and Wisconsin simply vanished into thin Biden leads.

At midnight on the evening of November 3, and as illustrated in Table 1, President Trump was ahead by more than 110,000 votes in Wisconsin and more than 290,000 votes in Michigan. In Georgia, his lead was a whopping 356,945; and he led in Pennsylvania by more than half a million votes. By December 7, however, these wide Trump leads would turn into razor thin Biden leads—11,779 votes in Georgia, 20,682 votes in Wisconsin, 81,660 votes in Pennsylvania, and 154,188 votes in Michigan.

Table 1: A Trump Red Tide Turns Biden Blue

	GEORGIA	PENNSYLVANIA	MICHIGAN	WISCONSIN
Trump Lead Midnight 11/3	356,945	555,189	293,052	112,022
Biden "Lead" 12/15	11,779	81,660	154,188	20,682

Sources: Associated Press & Edison/Decision Desk HQ
*Midnight based on state's time zone

There was an equally interesting story unfolding in Arizona and Nevada. While Joe Biden was ahead in these two additional battleground states on election night—by just more than

30,000 votes in Nevada and less than 150,000 votes in Arizona—internal Trump Campaign polls predicted the president would close these gaps once all the votes were counted. Of course, this never happened.

In the wake of this astonishing reversal of Trump fortune, a national firestorm erupted over the fairness and integrity of one of the most sacrosanct institutions in America—our presidential election system. Critics on the Right and within the Republican party—including President Trump himself—have charged that the election was stolen. They have backed up these damning charges with more than fifty lawsuits, thousands of supporting affidavits and declarations, and seemingly incriminating videos, photos, and first-hand accounts of all manner of chicanery.

Critics on the Left and within the Democratic party have, on the other hand, dismissed these charges as the sour grapes of a whining loser. Some of these critics have completely denied any fraud, misconduct, or malfeasance altogether. Others have acknowledged that while some election irregularities may have existed, they strenuously insist that these irregularities are not significant enough to overturn the election.

There was a similar Battle Royale raging between large anti-Trump segments of the so-called "mainstream" media and alternative conservative news outlets. Across the anti-Trump mainstream media diaspora—which includes most prominently print publications like the *New York Times* and *Washington Post* and cable TV networks like CNN and MSNBC—a loud chorus of voices has been demanding that President Trump concede the election.

These same anti-Trump voices have been equally quick to denounce or discredit anyone—especially anyone within their own circle—that dares to investigate what may well turn out to be THE biggest political scandal in American history. Social media outlets like Facebook, Twitter, and YouTube likewise have been actively and relentlessly censoring anyone who dares to call the results of the election into question.

In contrast, alternative news outlets, primarily associated with the American conservative movement, have provided extensive, in-depth coverage of the many issues of fraud, misconduct, and other irregularities that are coming to light. From Steve Bannon's War Room Pandemic and John Solomon's Just the News, to Raheem Kassam's National Pulse to Newsmax and One America News Network, Americans hungry for facts and breaking developments have been able to find such critical information only by following this alternative coverage.

That the American public is not buying what the Democratic party and the anti-Trump media and social media are selling is evident in public opinion polls. For example, according to a recent Rasmussen poll: "Sixty-two percent (62%) of Republicans say it is 'Very Likely the Democrats stole the election'" while 28% of Independents and 17% of Democrats share that view.

If, in fact, compelling evidence comes to light proving the election was indeed stolen after a *fait accompli* Biden inauguration, we as a country run the very real risk that the very center of our great American union will not hold.

To put this another way: If the greatest democracy in world history cannot conduct a free and fair election, and if much of the mainstream media of this country won't even fully investigate what is becoming a growing mountain of evidence calling into question the election result, there is little chance that our democracy and this Republic will survive as we know it. It is therefore critical that we get to the bottom of this matter. That is the purpose of the Navarro Report.

Evidence used in the preparation of the Navarro Report includes more than fifty lawsuits and judicial rulings, thousands of affidavits and declarations, testimony in a variety of state venues, published analyses by think tanks and legal centers, videos and photos, public comments, and extensive press coverage.

	ARIZONA	GEORGIA	MICHIGAN	NEVADA	PENNSYLVANIA	WISCONSIN
Outright Voter Fraud	√	√	*	√	*	√
Ballot Mishandling		√	√	√	√	√
Contestable Process Fouls	√	√	√	√	√	√
Equal Protection Clause Violations	√	√	√	√	√	√
Voting Machine Irregularities	√	√	√	√	√	*
Significant Statistical Anomalies	√	√	√	√		√

√ = Wide-Spread Evidence · * = Some Evidence

Volume One finds significant election irregularities across six key battleground states—Arizona, Georgia, Michigan, Nevada, Pennsylvania, and Wisconsin. These irregularities, noted in the chart, range from outright voter fraud, ballot mishandling, and contestable process fouls to Equal Protection Clause violations, voting machine irregularities, and significant statistical anomalies.

From the findings of Volume One, it is possible to infer what may well have been a coordinated strategy to effectively stack the election deck against the Trump-Pence ticket. Indeed, the observed patterns of election irregularities are so consistent across the six battleground states that they suggest a coordinated strategy to, if not steal the election outright, strategically game the election process in such a way as to "stuff the ballot box" and unfairly tilt the playing field in favor of the Biden-Harris ticket.

Volume Two examines a two-pronged Grand "Stuff the Ballot Box" Strategy used by the Democratic party and its political operatives to flood the battleground states with enough illegal absentee and mail-in ballots to turn a decisive Trump victory into a narrow and arguably illegitimate Biden "win." To strategically game the presidential election, the Democrats and their operatives were found to have at times bent or broken both election rules and laws.

Volume Three provides the most up-to-date statistical "receipts" with respect to the potential number of illegal votes cast in each battleground state. Volume Three thereby provides investigators with a well-documented tally of potentially illegal votes on a state-by-state and category-by-category basis. A key finding is that the number of potentially illegal votes dwarfs the very thin alleged Biden "victory" margins across all six battleground states.

To read this report is to understand at a granular and evidentiary level why the insurrection charges against President Donald J. Trump must be dismissed. These highly partisan charges are absurd on their face and an affront to the more than 74 million patriotic Americans who voted for President Trump.

Appendix B: President Trump's First Term Border Security Achievements

Author's Note: On the eve of the pandemic, in February 2020, I penned a White House report entitled "The Causes and Costs of Illegal Immigration through the United States' Southwest Border." This report is useful for the purposes of this book because, among other things, it provides a useful summary of the specific actions taken by President Trump to secure our southern border.

These actions are summarized in this appendix and it thereby helps set the stage for a second Trump term of, as Steve Bannon often says, "Action, action, action!" You can access the full report at www.peternavarro.com

Illegal migration vexed the United States for decades. Donald Trump prevailed in 2016 largely on a promise to finally confront this massive threat to America's sovereignty and prosperity. His first term accomplishments proved the efficacy of smart, tough policies regarding immigration and border defense.

However, with a Biden presidency, powerful interests have aligned to roll back the Trump progress and regress to an era of porous borders and nearly open-ended migration into America. Such a retreat will reward big business seeking cheap labor and the Democratic party luring new constituents. A massive new inflow of migrants, both legal and illegal, is already bringing grave harm to working-class Americans, lowering wages, inflicting gigantic costs upon taxpayers, and jeopardizing U.S. national security.

Regrettably, Biden finds many allies among establishment Republicans in his efforts to open our borders. Some in Congress, like Senator Marco Rubio, openly cooperate with George Soros–backed groups pushing mass amnesty for illegal aliens. In contrast, patriotic leaders of the America First movement push back against such dangerous posturing.

It is well worth cataloguing and remembering just exactly how President Trump brought long overdue reform to American immigration policy, enabling the nation to finally enjoy the protection and prosperity that strong and secure borders provide. Through a series of executive actions, agency-level changes, and even international cooperation, the massive inflow of illegal aliens had been substantially curtailed as President Trump introduced novel and innovative improvements to protect American citizens.

Trump's four pillars for immigration reform were introduced in his first State of the Union address:

(1) increased border security and funding; (2) ending the di-

versity visa lottery; (3) restrictions on family-based immigration; and (4) a path to citizenship for DREAMers.

Presidential Actions

Within his first week in office, President Trump introduced an executive order reprioritizing the removal of illegal aliens who have been convicted of *any* criminal offense. Previous administrations had permitted lawlessness and criminal behavior of any level committed by illegal aliens, excluding serious crimes. This essential pivot marked a new day in immigration policy and the security of the United States.

Wasting no time, the Buy American, Hire American Executive Order was issued months later, ending the federal government's neglect of American workers for cheaper, temporary foreign labor. Within a year, U.S. Citizenship and Immigration Services embarked upon sweeping actions to protect U.S. workers and their wages. The Trump administration also increased transparency and fraud detection efforts in employment-based visa programs.

Also responding to the President's EO, the Justice Department launched the Protecting U.S. Workers Initiative to target, investigate, and hold accountable companies that intentionally discriminate against American workers in favor of cheaper foreign labor via temporary visa programs. As of March 2020, the Initiative had reached settlements with eight different companies found illegally prioritizing temporary visa workers over Americans and garnered more than $1.2 million in penalties and back pay to affected U.S. workers.

Most notable, however, is the president's commitment to build a wall along the southern border to finally end the rampant and unrestrained border crossing of millions of illegal aliens. In February 2019, the problem worsened so dramatically that the president declared a national emergency to secure $8 billion in funding, the first time since 9/11 that an emergency declaration authorized military action. By the end of 2020, more than 450 additional miles of the U.S.-Mexico border wall were completed. To expedite the mission, 4,000 National Guard personnel were sent to the southern border to support federal border security and wall construction efforts.

To enhance domestic screening and vetting requirements of foreign nationals desiring to enter the United States, the president created the National Vetting Center. By creating an information-sharing apparatus, the Department of Homeland Security was finally able to automatically check the names of foreigners seeking to enter the United States with other intelligence agencies and highly classified databases. These higher levels of interagency cooperation enabled unprecedented levels of coordination and information sharing to assist our law enforcement officers and other federal government workers in securing our borders.

President Trump also lowered the unnecessarily high ceiling for refugee admissions as many of the extenuating conflicts that justified these levels have been sufficiently resolved. Since 2016, this admissions ceiling had been reduced by more than 75 percent (84,994 in FY16; 18,000 in FY20), eliminating the program's rampant abuse.

Many who come to the United States, whether as refugees or legal aliens, remain in the country beyond the allotted time and can live in America unnoticed for years or even decades, leeching benefits from citizen welfare programs without ever contributing to them. Recognizing this grim reality, President Trump restricted visa access to foreign nationals from countries with high visa overstay rates in order to prevent future overstays.

As of March 2019, 415,000 foreign nationals were estimated to be living in the United States beyond their nonimmigrant visa time allotment. Scofflaws from twenty nations exhibit overstay rates exceeding 10 percent, and some countries have rates of up to 30, or even 40 percent. This unrestrained exploitation of the generosity and good will of the United States was finally curtailed under the Trump administration.

In May 2019, President Trump issued a Memorandum on Enforcing the Legal Responsibilities of Sponsors of Aliens. In doing so, the president ordered the enforcement of financial commitments of immigrant sponsors who pledge to reimburse the government should the immigrants they sponsor receive public benefits.

The global pandemic necessitated additional reform in immigration policy to protect the American people. As the CCP virus spread, restricting travel became an expedient, essential move.

To secure our borders from the CCP virus, President Trump swiftly banned non-citizens traveling from China and shortly thereafter terminated entry of persons from thirty-one countries, including travel restrictions with Mexico and Canada. President Trump also terminated new immigrant and nonimmigrant work visas through the year 2020 in order to prioritize American workers in the recovering job market, creating an estimated 525,000 jobs for Americans.

In March 2020, on grounds of public health, the Centers for Disease Control invoked Section 362 of the Public Health Service Act, temporarily terminating the introduction of persons or goods into the United States. This move suspended asylum claims at the southern border.

The president also signed an executive order in April 2020, temporarily suspending the approval of green cards, particularly green card holders sponsoring their extended families for permanent U.S. residency, also known as chain migration. Additionally, the Diversity Visa Lottery was suspended. Looking to ameliorate potential future impacts of illegal immigration, the president eliminated illegal aliens for apportionment purposes in the 2020 Census. This move alone prevented an estimated 14.3 million illegal aliens from skewing apportionment intended to be based on U.S. *citizens.*

As evidenced, President Trump dynamically and effectively exercised the powers available to him to reform immigration policy and to protect the United States. Illegal aliens hiding in the United States were being removed *en masse.* Under President Trump, the once steady stream of illegal migration was largely curtailed. While using the full measure of his executive power, President Trump also directed various agencies and departments to respond in their jurisdictions to curb the pervasive and pernicious threat of illegal immigration.

A: Agency Authority and Policy Changes

At the direction of the president, myriad agencies adjusted protocols, procedures, and policies to curb the entry of illegal aliens into the United States. An assortment of major policy changes is detailed below.

Temporary Protected Status (TPS)

Migrants from countries that have experienced severe conflict, natural disasters, or other forms of extenuating unrest may be designated with temporary protected status (TPS). Initially, Congress established this legal status in 1990 to provide asylum for Salvadorans impacted by their civil war. The designation permits TPS individuals to reside in the United States for up to eighteen months and can be renewed as seen fit. From 2017 to 2019, TPS designation terminated for Sudan, Nicaragua, Haiti, El Salvador, Honduras, and Nepal, as conflicts and protracted unrest in these areas have been sufficiently resolved for the safe return of their citizens. Former TPS designees then receive twelve to eighteen months to plan for their repatriation.

Prompt Asylum Care Review (PACR) and Humanitarian Asylum Review Program (HARP)

These two novel programs aimed to alleviate and expedite the immense backlog of asylum cases that were formerly under the exclusive competency of ICE, but now receive CBP support. Humanitarian claims were adjudicated more efficiently and humanely as those who do not meet the standards were removed swiftly, within ten days.

Transit-Country Asylum Ban

More commonly known as third-country agreements, transit-country asylum bans reduced fraudulent claims of asylum, nearly cutting the approved rates in half from 80 percent to 45 percent from June to December 2019. A migrant crossing through a third country en route to the U.S.-Mexico border who failed to show evidence of a denied asylum application in at least one of these third countries was no longer eligible to receive asylum in the United States.

Narrowed Asylum Criteria

To be granted asylum, an individual must demonstrate that they have suffered or have well-founded fear of persecution on grounds of race, nationality, political opinion, and/or membership in a particular social group. In August 2014, in the *Matter of A-R-C-G*, the Justice Department's Board of Immigration Appeals significantly expanded the meaning of "membership in a particular social group" to "married women in Guatemala who are unable to leave their relationship" and who are victims of domestic abuse. With this ruling, the Board further opened the door to dubious asylum claims. Anyone making such a claim was previously released into the interior of the United States while awaiting adjudication of the matter.

Former Attorney General Sessions overruled this decision in 27 I&N Dec. 316 (A.G. 2018), eliminating gang or domestic violence from qualifying as "membership in a particular social group." However, this reform was stymied by a permanent injunction on December 19, 2018, by the U.S. District Court for the District of Columbia, in *Grace v. Whitaker.*

Public Charge Rule

Implemented by USCIS in February 2020, the public charge rule restricts admission to any immigrant who will become a net burden to the taxpayer. Unlike many other administration actions, the public charge rule has existed in immigration law in various forms for more than one hundred years.

To determine if a migrant may become a net burden, various

factors are evaluated, including age, health, family status, education, skills, assets, and ability to speak English. Generally speaking, this litmus test means individuals applying for visas must have a healthy income above the Federal Poverty Guideline, a good credit score, health insurance, have employment or recent employment, a minimum of a high school education or verified occupational skills, good health, no medical issues, and the ability to speak English. This policy ensures that the hard-earned tax dollars of American citizens are protected and that those entering our country to work or eventually become citizens will contribute just as every other American does.

Migrant Protection Protocols

In January 2019, migrant protection protocols were implemented allowing CBP to return migrants to Mexico to await their U.S. immigration court hearings and final adjudication. Previously, migrants were admitted into the United States and would enjoy lengthy waiting periods before their cases were heard, taking advantage of welfare programs in the meantime or never appearing for their hearings whatsoever, instead illegally hiding in the United States.

Fraudulent Families Initiative

ICE began the Fraudulent Families Initiative to identify migrants attempting to illegally obtain entry into the country with children they claim as their own, though are actually not relatives. Due to former leniencies regarding family immigration, those attempting to enter the United States have been incentivized to cross as families, real or not, jeopardizing the lives of thousands of children. Since the program's inception in April 2019, 238 fraudulent families have been identified, 329 false documents have been seized, 50 individuals have been identified who fraudulently claim to be UACs, and more than 350 individuals have been federally prosecuted.

DNA Collection

In 2005, the DNA Fingerprint Act was passed, calling for the collection of DNA samples, including fingerprints and cheek swabs, for those taken into custody by law enforcement officers. The Department of Justice implemented the act in 2009, though DHS received an exemption for non-criminal arrestees for one year in order to receive more time for its implementation.

This initial one-year extension was exploited and exhausted for the past decade, crippling CBP and ICE from being able to identify a potentially dangerous criminal among the nearly one million illegal aliens who have been detained and released. At the direction of President Trump, Attorney General Barr issued a Final Rule ordering DHS to collect DNA samples from detainees. Finally, our law enforcement officers had access to DNA sampling that enabled them to identify subjects, connect suspects to crimes, and eliminate criminal illegal aliens from our borders.

B: Cooperation with Foreign Nations

President Trump also directed various agencies to work with foreign governments. Trump reduced our reliance on flimsy and hollow international immigration agreements, such as the

Global Compact on Migration, and instead took proactive steps to strengthen American policy and correct international expectations.

Trump discouraged illegal entry into the United States by removing incentives, loopholes, and free-rides in immigration policy. His administration also assisted our Central American neighbors in developing a prosperous, vibrant region where their people feel safe and optimistic creating futures in their own countries. Protecting Americans and their interests is the first priority of this administration. However, discouraging individuals of any nation from risking their lives with nefarious smugglers and criminal organizations seeking to obtain illegal entry into the United States is also a victory that protects peoples everywhere.

In the latter half of 2019, a series of cooperative efforts were launched with the nations of the Northern Triangle—Honduras, El Salvador, and Guatemala. These include Asylum Cooperative Agreements (ACAs), Border Security Arrangements, and Biometric Data Sharing Program (BDSP) Arrangements.

In FY2019, more than 72 percent of all apprehended migrants at the U.S.-Mexico border came from Northern Triangle countries. ACAs were entered into with these countries, allowing migrants to seek protection in Central America instead of the United States. ACAs facilitate cooperation between the United States and host nation governments to enlarge humanitarian protections and return individuals to the Northern Triangle. The Biden-Harris Regime is dismantling these programs as well.

Biden's decision harms the Border Security Agreements that facilitated institutional knowledge, training, and tactics to be shared with our foreign partners in assisting their own efforts to secure borders and resolve migratory challenges. ICE and CBP officials were deployed to tutor and aid host nation law enforcement officials in police, immigration, and border security forces.

Indeed, BDSP Arrangements significantly improved cooperation between Northern Triangle nations and DHS by proliferating information sharing and biometric data collection. As this crucial information is shared between partners, counterparts in both nations can better prevent and combat crime and resolve other threats to public and national security. Irregular migrant identities can more frequently and efficiently be identified and verified, enabling enhanced detection of wanted criminals, smugglers, and international criminal organizations. Another program known as Electronic Nationality Verification (ENV) enables repatriation of Central American migrants lacking fear claims to return to their countries of origin in a more expedited manner.

Trump also invoked Section 243(d) of the Immigration and Nationality Act (INA), suspending issuance of visas to nations denying or unreasonably delaying repatriation of their citizens ordered to be removed from the United States. "Visa sanctions" were imposed on Cambodia, Eritrea, Guinea, and Sierra Leone in 2017; Laos and Burma in 2018; Pakistan, Cuba, and Ghana in 2019.

The administration also maintained high levels of cooperation with Mexico to disrupt transnational criminal organizations, in turn disrupting human trafficking and smuggling efforts in the Americas and around the globe. During the pandemic, the two governments coordinated military and law enforcement personnel along the southern border to ensure the health and safety of both nations.

Conclusion

This summary demonstrates that the Secure Border policies of the Trump Administration made tremendous inroads into combating the problems associated with illegal immigration. If the president had won a second term—and given the widespread election irregularities fully documented in the *Navarro Report*, many people believe he did—the Trump policies, together with the president's completed border wall, would have gone a long way toward ending America's battle with an issue that continues to sharply divide the American people.

While the Democratic party ostensibly represents the working poor and blue-collar laborers of America, this political party now advocates unrelentingly for open borders that will afflict maximum damage to these constituencies.

In all likelihood, the Democratic party pushes for open borders in the belief that these illegal immigrants will eventually support the Democratic party once afforded citizenship and vote for lasting Democratic control of both Congress and the White House. This calculus may well prove false as President Trump experienced some of his biggest improvements in vote totals among Blacks and Hispanics who have borne the brunt of the Democrats' open border policies.

As the Biden-Harris Regime continues to dismantle the Secure Order policies of the Trump administration, and as a crisis on our southern border gains in intensity, it is well worth remembering that elections have consequences. On our southern border, the very worst is yet to come—we must brace for the fallout.

Visit WinningPublishing.com and stay up to date on our newest releases!

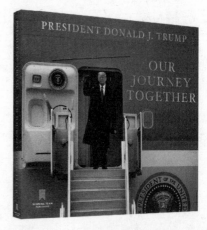

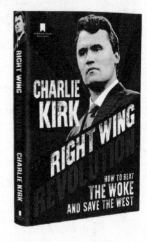